PRAISE FOR (

'I thought I set the record for the most failures versus successes. Then I met Fred. The great advantage Fred has over me is his failures have been far less expensive and his successes, especially Finder, have been way, way bigger than what I could achieve. Fred's book is human, funny, thought-provoking and most of all inspires you, even 'has-beens' like me. I haven't enjoyed reading a book on business as much as I have reading this. Read Fred's book and you too could look forward to many failures – and one massive success that will make up for all of them.'

John Singleton, entrepreneur

'It takes guts to start a business; it takes even more courage to tell people the truth about the journey. Fred captures the challenges of entrepreneurship and global aspirations in a frank and transparent way. If you have ever wanted to know what it is like to be an entrepreneur, *Go Live!* is for you.'

Naomi Simson, Founder of RedBalloon and
Shark Tank Australia shark

'Put your carry-on emotional baggage in the locker above your seat and set your biases to permanent flight mode. Prepare for take-off on a fun, informative and brutally honest flight with one of the best in the business.'

Adam Spencer, MC, author and host of
The Big Questions on PodcastOne

'Startups are the lifeblood of the private sector, and those brave enough to at least try need all the support and fresh ideas they can get. Fred's book is simply bursting with smart tips and encouraging frameworks that are sure to enhance outcomes!'

Andrew Banks, entrepreneur, evangelist and
former shark on Shark Tank Australia

'A great leader is someone who can create other leaders. Fred defines this. His pure enthusiasm is inspirational, even to those who have already reached their success. His contribution to leadership, independence and creativity is something we all should strive for.'

Brock Pierce, US presidential candidate

'Fred Schebesta nails it in *Go Live! 10 Principles to Launch a Global Empire*. As we say at Draper University, "Fail and fail again until I succeed." Fred shows how a willingness to try things freely (and not wait for someone's permission – who has never seen anything like it before) is a great recipe for making a startup successful.'

Tim Draper, Founder of Draper Associates,
DFJ and Draper University

'I'm proud to have been a mentor for Fred. He has taken everything I showed him and made it shine. He is on his way to the moon, and *Go Live!* will allow anyone who has the drive and commitment to go there with him.'

Michael Kiely, Australian Direct Marketing
Association Hall of Fame inductee

'The first time I met with Fred, I was struck by his vision and ability to create great things. But more importantly, Fred can help guide humans to create great things on behalf of other humans. Fred gets the most important element of any human endeavour: answering the "why" of it all. If you want to learn how to create a sustainably great thing, Fred is the real deal to learn from.'

Allen Olivo, Senior Marketing Executive: Apple, Amazon,
Yahoo! and PayPal

'Fred's thinking about building a global empire is unmatched. He really is a pioneer in business growth, and these 10 principles will help any-one to Go Live. Highly recommended.'

Sam Cawthorn, CEO & Founder of Speakers Institute, international bestselling author and 2009 Young Australian of the Year for Tasmania

'Fred is a talented entrepreneur with a wealth of knowledge that he generously shares with others. Told in a straight-up, honest fashion, *Go Live!* teaches you very quickly which obstacles are your own and how to create a confident path to success! This is an inspiring book that challenges readers to step into their greatness, create their own rules and dare to take a chance on themselves.'

Christie Whitehill, Founder and Director of Tech Ready Women

'If you want to learn to build a startup, you need to find someone who's had the right mix of success and failure, and the honesty to discuss both sides of the journey. *Go Live!* is an engaging and honest look into the principles of startup life. I highly recommend it for anyone wanting to launch their startup journey.'

Kain Warwick, Founder of Synthetix.io

'In *Go Live!*, Fred Schebesta not only provides the mindset tools applicable to a budding startup entrepreneur but reveals in his loud, authentic and kind-but-to-the-point rebel manner that the key to all success in life and business is the investment you make in yourself. If you have a startup, and especially if you want to scale it internationally, Fred's principles in *Go Live!* will serve you very well!'

Flic Manning, author, speaker and Founder of Corethentic

'*Go Live!* plugs us into Fred's supercharged mind and reveals his crazy genius. Truly action-packed!'

Robert Gerrish, Founder of Flying Solo, author and presenter

'*Go Live!* is a must-read for any current or aspiring entrepreneurs. Fred's insight into the fundamentals of a startup is unmatched. For anyone lacking direction or looking to find a new light for their business, this book is for you.'

Taylor Reilly, 'a north star for entrepreneurs'

GO LIVE!

10 PRINCIPLES TO LAUNCH
A GLOBAL EMPIRE

Fred Schebesta

For Portia, Tsaatchi and Frëderick,
and their future families and beyond.
Dream wildly and uninhibited.
And to my love B.

First published in 2021 by Major Street Publishing Pty Ltd
E: info@majorstreet.com.au W: majorstreet.com.au M: +61 421 707 983

A catalogue record for this book is available from the National Library of Australia

Printed book ISBN: 978-1-922611-04-8
Ebook ISBN: 978-1-922611-05-5

Cover design by Tess McCabe
Cover image by Mike Belkin
Internal design by Production Works

Printed in Australia by IVE Group, an Accredited ISO AS/NZS 14001:2004 Environmental Management System Printer.

10 9 8 7 6 5 4 3 2 1

CONTENTS

PREFACE

As a startup, there is only one rule: there are no rules.

I want you to throw away any concept you've ever read or any idea you've ever studied that said there are certain rules you need to follow when you start a business. Take that book and burn it.

I could never write a book of 'rules' because I don't follow rules. I never have.

I break the rules.

And to be honest, I hope that's why you've ended up with *this* book in your hands, and why you've chosen me to come along for this wild ride. You think differently. You have an idea. Or at least, you want to learn how to develop one.

Rules are guidelines. I like to break rules because they are manufactured, imaginary ideas created by someone in a specific moment in time. They don't necessarily define the boundaries of what is possible and what is not. If you can interpret them and innovate around them, and work out how to get to the goal that normally lies beyond the rules, that's where growth and innovation happens.

Startups don't have rules. Every step they take is about creating. The Wright brothers didn't have a regulated pilot's licence when they were out there building, testing and flying the first ever motor-operated airplane.

There are no rules, but there are principles.

Principles are eternal ideas and philosophies. This is my fundamental truth and it helps me in every decision I make. And that, in turn, creates success.

Anything is possible. There is no limit. There are no restrictions. Your only limitations are your belief in yourself and your idea.

So, what do I know? Well, a little.

I've been where you are now, with the seed of an idea – something I truly believed in – that I wanted to take to the next level. And I have, successfully. A few times.

Over more than 20 years of building businesses, I've failed more times than I've succeeded, and I'm ready to share my journey with you. This book is a collection of my highs and my lows, my best stories, my biggest fails and my favourite resources.

Each of the 10 chapters is about an eternal principle I follow when I'm taking a new venture from zero to 100. But they're more than that. These are the principles that I live by in my pursuit of hyper success.

I've written this book to help you build great companies that last for thousands of years. I want to inspire and challenge you to be the greatest creative version of yourself.

Disclaimer: I can teach you my 10 principles, but I need you to provide the determination, the persistence, the commitment and, above all, the grit.

Our end goal is to Go Live with your business idea. It's the namesake of this book and something I live by. I have an ingrained bias to Go Live! And I want to pass that onto you. We're executing ideas, we're putting things on the internet and we're turning dreams into reality. It's time to get right up there!

So, what are you waiting for?

PRINCIPLE 1

Grow outside of your comfort zone

⚡

'If we wait until we're ready,
we'll be waiting the rest of our lives.'

LEMONY SNICKET (AKA DANIEL HANDLER)

THIS IS YOUR CAPTAIN SPEAKING. *As we prepare to take off, the seatbelt sign has now been activated and all electronics must be switched off and bags stowed away. You're set to launch your business, and it's gonna get bumpy!*

Let's start with some straight chat: you want your business to take off, right? Of course you do. No one launches a business in the hope it'll fail. But the truth about building a successful business is that, along the way, you have to be ready for some turbulence.

Actually… a *lot* of turbulence.

Starting a business is not easy. Running a business isn't easy, either. In fact, it's probably the most challenging thing you'll ever do in your entire life. I would know. I've started many businesses. And I'll be real with you: most of them have failed.

But one of them is doing alright…

Finder started out as a student credit card blog that I wrote when I was trying to compare cards back in 2006. Today, it's one of the biggest comparison websites in the world, worth around half a billion Australian dollars at the time of writing.

Look, it's a comparison site, and you could say a comparison site is pretty boring at its core. It's not like we're matching people up with the future love of their life, or streaming *Game of Thrones*. Comparing interest rates is not 'sexy'. It's not something people wake up on a Sunday morning itching to do. 'Yesssss! I've been looking forward to comparing deals, reading the fine print and applying for a loan all week!' said no one ever.

I understand all of that. But I also understand that Finder is about *so much more* than simply helping people compare a credit card or a home loan rate. It exists to help connect people to a better financial future – one where they're in the driver's seat.

I've grown Finder (and some other businesses) over the past 22 years, and during that time I've mastered the art of developing, launching and scaling business ideas. In this book, I'm excited to share with you some of my hard-won principles from over the last two decades. I hope to inspire you to take that leap of faith towards building something epic!

But first, I have to warn you: some of these chapters may be confronting. Some will go deep into your core and might trigger your darkest fears. You might want to curl into a foetal position or bury your business idea in the backyard. It's okay to feel scared. It's okay to second-guess yourself. This is what building a business is all about.

ONE IN 40 BUSINESS IDEAS *MIGHT* WORK

Success isn't something I woke up with one day. It's something I've worked really, really hard at, year after year. And while I do feel as if I've achieved some success, I also treat every day as Day One.

Rewind 15 years and it's me and my business partner, Frank Restuccia, sitting in the kitchen of our share house. I call him Ciao to this day because back then, every day he would come home from his first job and I would be working on my computer. I would yell out, 'Ciao!', which is 'hi' in Italian. It was my way of welcoming him home.

We were starting all over again. We had just spent three years building, and then selling, a digital marketing agency called Freestyle Media. It taught us a lot about creating websites, marketing, search engine optimisation (SEO) and bringing in customers over the internet. We drank a lot of coffee and ate a lot of tinned spaghetti.

We learnt how to work hard and how to keep our heads above water – to keep the cash flow coming in and reduce the expenses going out. Business 101. We made so many mistakes. It was a brutal experience of struggle, survival and some success.

After we sold Freestyle Media, something shifted. We realised that instead of doing all the heavy lifting for other companies – creating websites and generating buzz for *others* – we could put the skills we'd developed towards something incredible for us, something with purpose that we could create for ourselves.

We started with 40 different business ideas. Thirty-nine of them failed. This was an exercise in getting hit, falling down, reflecting, learning and then ultimately carrying on.

Among the 40 different business ideas, we launched a poker site called 'Poker Champion', which sold poker tables and chips. We also had a sudoku site, but we couldn't figure out how to make money with it.

We bought a few domain names. One was anzacday.com.au. We made an enemy of a local radio station, which demanded we give the domain to the RSL clubs. We handed it over. We also bought the domain name christmasday.com.au, but that was no good because Christmas only comes around once a year.

Then, Finder was born.

At first, it was called Credit Card Finder. It was a single webpage that compared just two credit cards. But it felt right, and it's the first time I remember sitting at that kitchen table with Ciao feeling really happy.

We were building our own website instead of building one for other people. Even better, we were helping people. We were giving people the power to make better financial decisions.

TWO STEPS FORWARD, ONE STEP BACK

So, we'd planted these 40 seeds, and just one of them broke through the soil and started to bud. We gave that small bud a little more attention, and we watered it a little more. We watched it closely and we experimented with it. We listened to what it needed: more light, less light, a bigger or smaller pot. Finder was blooming into this magic beanstalk that we could use to climb all the way up to success.

Eventually, this one webpage became two, then five. We started comparing different types of credit cards, and then we compared home loans and savings accounts. We hit the top of Google search results for some key search terms. As a result, more people came to the site. It started with a few people, which became hundreds and then thousands. We started in one country, then a decade later we launched in two and then many more.

Success at this level starts with small, incremental changes every single day. I changed the design of the site, wrote articles and brought clients on board. I built a credit card debt repayment calculator, and I promoted the site on social media. I basically did all the things that we still do today, just on a much smaller scale.

What I discovered very early on is that starting a business is not a linear process. There is no right way to do it and there is no 'proven' method for successful results or outcomes.

There is no knowing for sure at what point you will stumble, or fall, or need to start over. Your success as an entrepreneur lies in being okay with that. You need to always be slightly uncomfortable, because that is how you will grow.

And *that* is my first principle to Go Live!

Going live is about embracing that feeling of the unknown – the anxiety of walking in darkness without a clear path laid out in front of you, of not knowing where the road will take you or if this risk will pay off.

'If you don't try, if you don't challenge yourself, you will never realise what you're truly capable of.'

Fred Schebesta

Success is about starting with a formula and applying it, and adapting until something breaks through and gains a little momentum. Follow that trail of breadcrumbs and keep iterating. It might not be your first idea that takes off; it might be the 40th thing you try!

YOU DON'T BECOME A COWBOY WITHOUT A FEW METEOR SHOWERS

When I'm hit with a setback – and running a company the size of Finder, there are plenty – Ciao often says to me, 'You don't become a cowboy without a few meteor showers.'

Here's a story about one of those storms...

It was 2016 and I was sitting in our newly rented (and very empty) office on East Broadway in Chinatown, Manhattan, New York City. I was by myself, and it was very late at night.

After growing Finder to the top of the market in Australia, this was our first attempt to expand overseas. Not just anywhere, mind you, but the United States – one of the biggest potential expansion markets on the planet!

For this to work, I knew we needed to recruit an incredible crew. So, I wrote some job ads and advertised the roles on all the big job sites. I had job ads everywhere – but *no* applications were coming in. As in, zero. None!

At first, I wondered if it was because Finder was a brand-new startup in the US. We were an unproven brand – a tiny fish

'CREATIVITY IS MAKING MONEY OUT OF THE IMAGINARY.'

FRED SCHEBESTA

swimming in a very, very big pond. Perhaps people were scared to work with us? I didn't want to subscribe to that idea, because I knew deep down that we had something great to offer, but I have to admit: it was humbling.

I don't give in to fear without a fight, so I dug deep for solutions. I tweaked the copy of the ad (to be honest, I tried every copywriting hack in the book). I triple-checked that the sign-up process was working. I even called the technology company and ran them through the problem. Why wasn't I getting any bites? They couldn't help me. I'm pretty sure no one had ever called them before with that issue.

I checked the page was accessible on different devices. I rewrote the ad, again. Still, no emails. No applications. My inbox was barren.

I felt genuinely defeated. That night, I was a mess. I was used to experiencing a certain amount of success with Finder in Australia, but here I was on the other side of the planet, wallowing in failure.

In that moment, it truly felt like I was failing. Sure, I was committed – but was that really enough? I was no longer certain. I was starting to doubt myself.

It was a strange feeling to be standing at the top of a mountain – the comparison industry in Australia – for so long, then to realise I was standing on a mound of dirt looking up at Mount Everest: the comparison market in the US.

I was overwhelmed.

I called Ciao. I told him how I was struggling to get the US business off the ground. 'I don't think we are going to make it here,' I confessed. 'I can't even get anyone to come and work for us.'

I was at rock bottom. Honestly, I felt ready to tap out, to pull the plug on the US expansion and return to my much more familiar and comfortable playground in Australia with my tail between my legs.

'Schebesta,' Ciao said to me, 'here's the thing. If there's anyone in this world who can figure this out, it's you. I back you. You've got to keep going.'

His faith in me and his words in that moment were exactly what I needed. They weren't going to make a tonne of qualified job applications magically appear in my inbox, but they were a reminder that I hadn't come all this way to throw in the towel. I didn't know what the next step was going to be, but I refused to give up.

Next, I ran the problem past Jeremy Cabral, our Global Chief Operating Officer and a co-founder of Finder (I call him Bomber because he drops metaphorical bombs on the internet). Bomber is a very strategic thinker and a brilliant problem-solver. After I explained the conundrum, he thought for a few moments.

'Have you checked your spam?' he said.

Spam. BOOM! How had I not thought to look there?!

As soon as I clicked on the folder, I realised my inbox had been flooded with hundreds of applications. I was *ecstatic*. I was shouting and jumping around the room with glee.

'We're back, baby!'

Within a week, our office turned into Grand Central at peak hour. We had a revolving door of people coming in and out for interviews. It was full steam ahead. Our founding US team was built, and we carried on.

It was just another meteor shower. These moments are hard, but on the other side you will always come out stronger, more resilient and ready to take on the next challenge. Because there will always be more.

THE GRIT TO GO LIVE!

Ciao and I didn't take a salary from Finder for the first two years. We poured everything we had into the business and invested every dollar we made back in.

We did absolutely everything we could to stay afloat. We rented out rooms in our share house before Airbnb was a thing. We went to free events and loaded up on the food so we didn't have to go home to another night of tinned spaghetti. It was brutal. But it was worth it.

Success wasn't just when I discovered the spam folder full of job applications that night in New York City back in 2016. Success was all the moments leading up to that point, good and bad; it was every time I pushed through and decided not to give up.

If you're reading this book while on the floor of your newly rented office, or at your kitchen table, or wherever you may be, I hope it gives you the gentle push you need to check your metaphorical spam folder and find all those reasons you *can* start your own business.

Perhaps you're sick of feeling restricted and unsatisfied in your job, and you're bursting with ideas for things that you could start creating – whether that's on your own or inside your organisation.

Maybe you're one of those people who have always dreamed of working for yourself. You're obsessed with the success stories of others who are living out their dreams. You follow countless experts online and listen to podcasts, watch videos and read blogs about business tips.

You have a good idea but have no idea where to start. The idea of quitting your day job gives you hives, and you feel so overwhelmed with the unknowns of running your own business that you keep putting it off.

Or perhaps you're a stay-at-home parent who feels like you've lost your identity and sense of purpose since you stopped working. Finally, the kids have started school, so you can no longer use the excuse that you don't have time to start the side hustle that you've been thinking about and putting off.

Maybe you have even started a business or two, but they have fizzled out for reasons you don't quite understand. You're keen to start again, but your past mistakes and lack of success have deflated your confidence.

For whatever reason, you've picked up this book. Whatever situation you find yourself in, I want to be your Ciao, your cheerleader telling you that you can do it when you think you can't. And I'm going to share with you how I did it, too.

READY TO GO LIVE? READ THIS FIRST

Wondering why I referred to myself as your 'captain' at the start of this chapter? I am in the business of launching metaphorical rocket ships: big ideas that blast off into space and make a difference. When rockets launch, they go straight up. And being 'straight up' transparent and honest is one of our core values at Finder.

I recently had some straight chat with one of my crew members. He was struggling with a particular problem and he wanted to give up. I told him, 'I refuse your can't.'

And guess what? I also refuse *your* can't.

Before we take off, there are a few people you need to get straight with: your customer, your team and yourself. Starting a business, making that business successful and ultimately becoming financially free is not for everyone. You need to understand the commitment and sacrifice it takes and be mentally prepared for the ride.

Straight chat isn't always hard to swallow. For example, here's some good news: there's never been a better time to start a business.

'RIGHT NOW, THE WORLD NEEDS CREATORS... SO WHAT ARE YOU GOING TO CREATE?'

FRED SCHEBESTA

Thanks to the COVID-19 pandemic, startups are finally on a level playing field with the big companies. Why? Because big companies are often janky, traditional and set in their ways. Startups are the opposite. They're agile and able to adapt – much faster, as well. Right now, the big companies are actually playing defence. As a startup, you're in a position to purely play the *offence*.

It's as though there is this wormhole that has opened up for you to climb through, to cut to the finish line. There are a million wormholes out there – you just need to find yours.

Take hand sanitiser, for instance. Aside from face masks, there wasn't a product as popular as hand sanitiser in 2020. A lot of companies started making hand sanitiser: breweries started turning their distilleries into hand sanitiser plants, and perfume companies started making it. There were incredible innovations happening inside companies all over the world.

Imagine the person inside that company who just said, 'Hey, we're going to survive,' and could see a different use for the conveyor belt. I love that.

While there were some clear winners of the pandemic, there were also some big losers. Some of the biggest ecommerce retailers and major websites in the world were broken. The cost of personal protective equipment products like hand sanitiser was inflated exponentially, and even the big sites couldn't keep up with the demand and were failing to weed out the scammers. Consumers were confused and scared and didn't know where to turn. I saw a wormhole.

We were business as usual at Finder, for the most part. After a short dip in traffic, the financial implications of the pandemic meant more people needed to compare their products to save some money. We worked hard to maintain our credibility with accurate content, so people continued to visit our websites. When I saw this wormhole, I went out to find some hand sanitiser to sell. A friend of mine was making it, so I asked him, 'Can we do a deal and I'll market your product?' He was keen, because at this point he couldn't get on Amazon and couldn't buy Google ads. A deal was done.

We sold 2520 hand sanitiser units in 12 hours on the Finder site. And that was just one small experiment. I had reached into the wormhole, put my hand through, felt around and thought, 'what is this thing?' and then pulled out some money, which I was able to put straight back into the company. Creativity is making money out of the imaginary.

You don't always know where exactly the rocket ship is going to land. When you start, you probably only have 30 percent of the information you'll need. This was and is often the case for us, too.

Even today, we reinvent ourselves and pivot constantly to ensure we're doing better every day and building a sustainable business that will exist for the next 100 years and beyond. That's evolution.

THERE WILL BE A LOT OF UNCERTAINTY

To be successful and create a lasting, innovative business, you need to get used to a level of uncertainty. It will exist from the get-go and it will never go away. I love trying things that no one has ever done before. It's how you learn, develop new skills and master your craft. I love experimenting and testing things out. While you won't have to love uncertainty to be successful, you will have to be comfortable with it.

Right now, the world needs creators. So much of what we know has been torn down by a deadly pandemic. Society is actively looking to the creators for answers. So, what are you going to create?

If you've got a plan and an idea, now is probably the greatest time ever to start pitching, because you're showing that you can deal with chaos, major disruptions and uncertainty. You're already ahead.

'IT'S NOT ABOUT THE CARDS YOU'RE DEALT, BUT HOW YOU PLAY THE HAND.'

RANDY PAUSCH

Either now or later, it's always going to take hard work. I learnt this very early in my life. I used to play competitive tennis as a kid. One afternoon I was playing a match, and I was wiped off the floor and out of the competition by another player. I was walking with my mum back to the car and I was crying. I couldn't understand how I had lost so badly.

Mum looked at me, and I can still remember the words that fell out of her mouth very clearly: 'Son, that kid practised more than you. He hit more balls than you, and you think you can just roll in and win when you're not practising as hard as he is?'

It's true in tennis and in any game, in business and in life: you get out what you put in. How much are you willing to put in? How hard are you going to train?

'Those who don't give up are the ones who tend to win.'

Fred Schebesta

BEFORE WE GO ANY FURTHER, HERE ARE SOME HARD TRUTHS ABOUT STARTING A BUSINESS

1. Know that small can be beautiful

Just because your business is small doesn't mean it's not great. Small businesses have agility on their side – the speed that the big companies don't have. And they can have super-sharp focus.

When Ciao and I first started Finder, we concentrated on credit cards. That was our niche, our wormhole. Once we had mastered that, we expanded to other things.

Some of the most successful businesses in the world are winners because they stayed small and mastered their craft. There's a tofu shop in Japan that's one of the oldest eateries in town. It's been around for over 100 years – probably more – and the only thing it sells is tofu. It doesn't even sell drinks. People come from miles away to eat its tofu. Its owners have mastered their menu and created a legendary product.

Another example is Pat's King of Steaks in Philadelphia, which claims to have invented the original steak sandwich in 1930. It still makes them today in the same shop. When we were in New York setting up our US business in 2016, Bomber was travelling to Philadelphia and found this sandwich shop. He brought me back a sandwich and it was the best I've ever eaten.

2. Get ready for rejection

Just as we launched 39 ideas before landing on lucky number 40, you will probably get 39 'no's before you get your 'yes'. Let the rejections fuel you to do better and to continue evolving your idea and mastering your pitch.

If people aren't saying 'no' then your idea is probably not that controversial. You want lots of noes and then, despite that, you want to have extreme conviction about what it is that you are doing.

Take that failure and rejection, and put it in your rocket as fuel to launch yourself further and faster. It is literally a gift, because it's basically the universe saying, 'no one else is going to come and do this,' which is exactly what you want!

3. Ask yourself: what will you sacrifice?

This is going to be a long journey, and you need to figure out what you're willing to sacrifice. I'm very aware of the deep commitment I've made to be an entrepreneur. This isn't just a one-time investment; it's a lifelong commitment.

Starting a business needs huge amounts of your personal life capital. This includes your:

· emotional capital
· mental capital

- physical health capital
- relationship capital
- financial capital.

All of the things that make you, you. My contention is, you need to invest a lot of your personal life capital from all of these areas, otherwise you're not going to make it.

4. Refuse to give up

The difference between people who make it and people who don't is their commitment to never giving up.

It's going to get hard. There will be big highs and lows. And the lows are brutal.

It's the grit to carry on, stay focused towards your goals and keep hustling that will see you succeed.

IN THREE, TWO, ONE...

Thank you for letting me come on this journey with you. I know you've probably felt like giving up a few times before this book landed in your lap. If you're in that place right now, I empathise with you. I have been there.

I want you to look inside yourself right now and ask: can I just be a little more courageous? I don't mean have some courage in what you're doing, I mean have some courage in *yourself*. It's time to lift!

As Randy Pausch famously stated in his book *The Last Lecture*, 'It's not about the cards you're dealt, but how you play the hand.' It's not about the problems you've got – we all have problems. It's what you're going to do about them.

In this book, I am going to take you on my journey of mistakes, learnings and successes, and show you how I co-founded one of the most successful Australian businesses – all without any funding.

I'm here to help you Go Live! To Go Live is one of our values at Finder and it's baked in all the way down to our core. It means to put it out into the world. I have an online course by the same name, where I teach my process of developing and launching business ideas. It might be something you're interested in learning about after you've read this book.

We're going to start by working on your mindset, because this is where it all begins. I'm going to help you get inspired and take you through the principles I live by that have helped me on my journey to hyper success. You're going to identify your super-powers, and find your purpose and the place where you will create your magic.

We have lift off!

YOUR COMMITMENT CONTRACT

One of the things I'm good at is creating a safe space for people to be challenged. So, here's my challenge to you: sign the following contract.

You're going to list all the areas in which you're willing to make sacrifices in order to succeed. Promise yourself you won't throw in the towel when things get tough. Agree that you'll embrace the setbacks.

And then sign it.

COMMITMENT CONTRACT

This Commitment Contract is made on [date] _____

Between [your full name] _____

And [your business name] _____

By signing this Commitment Contract, you agree to commit 100 percent to your business. You will not give up when things get tough. You will embrace setbacks and learn from your mistakes.

List the areas in which you are willing to make sacrifices in order to make this commitment:

_____

_____

_____

_____

_____

_____

_____

_____

_____

_____

_____

Signature _____

Full name _____

PRINCIPLE 2

Persistence is omnipotent

'The most certain way to succeed is always
to try just one more time.'

THOMAS EDISON

'I AM NOT GOOD ENOUGH.'

How many times has that thought run through your head? Six years ago, it was on a constant loop for me. Finder was hitting its stride, which surprisingly did nothing for the barrage of self-deprecating thoughts that underpinned nearly everything I did.

I wasn't just 'not good enough' to meet the company's success. I didn't think I was good enough in *any* respect. I'm talking not good enough as a leader, not good enough to deserve the money in my life, or the happiness, the relationships, my daughters.

I felt like the 'me' that was showing up every morning was a fraud.

It took me years and some serious soul-searching to overcome that voice in my head. Today, there are still days when I don't think that I am good enough.

The difference is that today, I know that it's okay. I am not good enough, and that's okay.

Mantras can be a powerful tool. However, a mantra must be backed by a belief. It is impossible to rewire your brain from 'I am not good enough' to 'it's okay to not be good enough' by simply telling yourself that. You have to really believe it.

So, how do you silence the nagging beliefs that you're just some guy who got lucky, someone who doesn't deserve to be in the position you find yourself in, or someone who, at the rate you're going, is going to sabotage everything you've worked so hard for?

For me, the turning point was meeting my emotional coach, Craig Hall. He was referred to me by a friend. I had no idea what to

'The Last Person to give up is usually the one who wins.'

FRED SCHEBESTA

expect, but I believe in manufactured serendipity and my curiosity meant I was intrigued about what he could offer. I just follow things and find out where they lead, and then make an assessment from there.

Killing the 'I'm not good enough' dialogue in my head was one of the first things we worked on. This belief ran deep, like most beliefs do. Not being good enough was something I believed about myself so reverently that if I had to compare its neural pathway in my brain to a vein in my body, it was a full-blown, life-giving, major artery. To cut it off was to unsubscribe from something I'd subconsciously held onto my whole life.

It was like finding out that your favourite superhero is actually a bad guy. And in fact, I probably attached some of my self-worth to the 'I'm not good enough' villain.

The good thing about being an entrepreneur is that you're forced to find the courage to try new things. Try, and probably fail – but the operative word is 'try'. So, that's what I did, and my attempts to change my way of thinking about myself were when I truly stepped into my success.

While I'm not a therapist, a psychologist or a guru, I am an entre-preneur, and I am okay with not being good enough all the time. I've also worked hard to get to a place where the negative thoughts in my head are no longer standing in the way of my potential.

My ultimate goal is hyper success. I've spent years studying the methods and practices of some of the best leaders in the world on my quest for personal and professional growth.

Just like I have overcome my self-limiting beliefs, I want to help you overcome yours. It starts with Principle 2: persistence is omnipotent.

The last person to give up is usually the one who wins.

THINK LIKE AN ENTREPRENEUR

A long time ago, a mentor of mine told me a quote by the 30th president of the US, Calvin Coolidge: 'Persistence and determination alone are omnipotent.'

Coolidge said, 'Nothing in the world can take the place of persistence. Talent will not; nothing is more common than unsuccessful men with talent. Genius will not; unrewarded genius is almost a proverb.'

This quote has stayed with me because it reinforces what it means to truly be an entrepreneur. It doesn't matter how clever you are or how good you are at something; if you're not persistent, you will fail. The end.

If you want to be an entrepreneur, you need to think like one. I submit that this is the secret to success, and it's what Stanford psychologist Dr Carol Dweck calls a 'growth' mindset over a 'fixed' mindset.

'Learning something new, something hard, sticking to things – that's how you get smarter,' Dweck says.

'Setbacks and feedback weren't about your abilities, they were information you could use to help yourself learn.'

On a fundamental level, what this means is that the cream that rises to the top are those who are consistently and actively seeking out criticism, failure and opportunities for growth. You can't be the best unless you're committed to challenging, changing and listening.

So, while the voices inside your head that tell you, 'I am not good enough' are not helpful, a little (actually, a lot) of feedback can be the difference between success and failure.

According to Dweck, when you have a fixed mindset, you have a fixed perception of your abilities and your negative beliefs are proven through your failures. But a growth mindset is the opposite;

'NOTHING IN THE WORLD CAN TAKE THE PLACE OF PERSISTENCE.'

CALVIN COOLIDGE

it's the belief that you can continually improve through trials and tribulations.

Author and renowned graphic designer Debbie Millman had this message for students at a San Jose State University graduation speech: 'We begin by worrying we aren't good enough, smart enough or talented enough to get what we want. Then we voluntarily live in this paralysing mental framework rather than confront our own role in this paralysis. Just the possibility of failing turns into a dutiful, self-fulfilling prophecy...'

A growth mindset gets you out of this 'you're doomed from the start' frame of mind and gives you the confidence you need to believe your talent and abilities can be developed.

The COVID-19 pandemic provided a really good way to understand these different mindsets. When the pandemic first hit in March 2020, entire cities around the world went into lockdown. It was incredibly challenging, there were setbacks, and a huge amount of effort was needed to re-evaluate the conditions and pivot.

Finder was not immune to this. We took a beating. We lost $2 million in revenue basically overnight. But we came together to find opportunities, curbed our spending and even launched new projects.

The pandemic showed us how to prepare for the unexpected. It proved that it is those who have a growth mindset – who embrace challenges and setbacks, who can adapt and pivot quickly – who ultimately build sustainable businesses.

You will achieve what you give yourself permission to believe, whether you call it a growth mindset, manifestation or the law of attraction. You're in the driver's seat and ultimately responsible for how high your rocket ship will fly.

'You can't reach hyper success without a growth mindset.'

Fred Schebesta

GROWING UP WITH A GROWTH MINDSET

When I was growing up, I always embodied a growth mindset, even though I wasn't conscious of it. Back then, they just called me a rebel. Either way, I knew I always wanted to do things differently.

School is a great example. I didn't love school. I didn't really apply myself until the very end. I preferred spending my days skateboarding, playing chess or mucking around with computers. I also loved climbing trees and starting fires. I still love starting fires, but more of the metaphorical kind. I think it's great to occasionally shake things up by challenging people to try something new, to see things from a different perspective.

I was a teacher's worst nightmare. I would often try to outsmart them in class. I knew where the line was, and sometimes I crossed it just to see what was on the other side. In my opinion, the rules were optional. Sometimes they needed to be broken; sometimes they weren't even there in the first place.

I love to explore, to create. Just like the trailblazers before me – the astronauts who went to space before there were borders, or the explorers who discovered new lands without passports, or the Wright brothers who built and flew the first motor-operated airplane without any money or college education.

While I wasn't a straight-A student in my early years at school, I did know that if I applied myself, I could beat the system. I was the kid who started studying right when push came to shove in my final year, and I did pretty well in the exams. I wanted to prove to everyone that I could.

I was the eldest son of two doctors. My father, Dr. Alfred Schebesta, is an anesthesiologist, and my mother, Dr. Kerrie Meades, is a leading ophthalmologist in Australia. Mum was the first female ophthalmologist to perform laser vision correction in Australia. My parents worked super hard raising me and my two sisters

'IF YOU
DO FEEL READY,
YOU'RE PROBABLY
LAUNCHING
TOO LATE.'

FRED SCHEBESTA

while studying to achieve great things in their own careers. My mother faced a lot of backlash studying medicine in the 1970s and 1980s while raising three children. She is the most courageous and determined person I know.

I grew up in a very high-achieving household, and to win any sort of argument I had to outsmart everyone. From a young age, I believed the best way to actually win an argument was to solve it in a different way that no one else would think of, and that's how I developed a lateral-thinking mindset.

BE YOUR OWN REBEL

My rebellious nature really fostered my growth mindset. As a kid, I did things on my own terms. I was told 'no' a lot. This made me challenge the reasons why I was told 'no' and figure out new ways of doing things. And today, I am still doing things in my own way.

A growth mindset is all about being inspired to try new things and learn from them, sometimes not giving a crap about the outcome (or whether you'll end up in trouble!). I live by the philosophy that it's better to beg for forgiveness than to ask for permission.

When I had my first business, I wore suits every day. However, after we sold Freestyle Media, I found a new level of confidence. Ciao and I proved to ourselves that we could launch a business and find success. We did it once and we were going to do it again. I didn't have to prove myself to anyone.

I remember the moment I decided I'd never wear a suit again. It's not that I have anything against them — they're just totally not my style. I was on Bondi Road driving home from work and I saw a dude wearing a suit with Converse High Tops on a skateboard. I thought this was the coolest get-up I'd ever seen. It made me take a look at myself and the expectations I had placed on myself to look a certain way.

I realised I didn't need to look like anyone else, and I had the power to decide how I wanted to present myself to the world.

The next day, I walked into the office and straight into a client meeting wearing jeans and a black leather jacket. Everyone in the room looked a little shocked. I sat down and told them what they had to do to reach their goal. And then I left the meeting.

Being the most authentic version of yourself is what's going to get attention. It's also what's likely to get criticised, but take your newly found growth mindset and welcome the criticism.

You can be remarkable with or without a suit.

TO BE EXTRAORDINARY, YOU CAN'T DO ORDINARY

I wasn't a business-minded kid. I didn't run lemonade stands or sell baseball cards in the schoolyard. But I did have the right mindset. I was curious.

I was curious about a lot of things, but especially computers. I'd go out and buy the latest RAM. I hacked them, pulled them apart and then put them back together. I configured my own machine. It wasn't for any particular reason – more so that I've always had a questioning nature and a niggling interest. That's still my attitude today.

I was kind of a sucky businessperson at the beginning of my career. However, I knew I wanted to do something extraordinary, and I wanted to *be* extraordinary. I pushed myself to grow and I wanted to learn as much as I could from all the knocks that came flying at me. I welcomed them.

Just like when my mum told me I wasn't going to win any tennis games without practising more than my opponents. Well, you'd better believe I started hitting some balls.

There's a concept you can trace back to a paper by Anders Ericsson from the University of Colorado in the 1990s. It says it takes 10,000 hours of deliberate practice to become an expert at anything.

> **'If you relentlessly pursue a goal, fall over, get back up and continue on your pursuit, eventually success is non-negotiable.'**
>
> Fred Schebesta

THE TIME IS RIGHT... NOW!

I live by the value of Go Live! And I encourage you to try it.

But I'm going to let you in on a little secret. You will probably never feel entirely ready to Go Live with your idea. In fact, if you do feel ready, you're probably launching too late.

Going live is a great practice in expanding your growth mindset: jump straight in there, and mess it up a few times. You have to be in it to win it. This is your first hour of 10,000, remember.

Call a meeting with the voices in your head – especially those who insist you are not ready – and listen to all the reasons you shouldn't start this project. Write them down, and then start right there. That's a perfect place to start.

> **'The best time to plant a tree was 20 years ago. The second best time is now.'**
>
> Chinese proverb

CHASING A GROWTH MINDSET

I am a pretty unusual person in that I have a lot of energy, and I channel that energy into ideas at all times of the day – and night. I'm often awake at 3am scribbling down notes when I'm inspired with an idea.

But like everyone, I go through periods of demotivation too. I get uninspired. I burn out and I hit a wall. I've fallen asleep in meetings and needed to double down on my exercise just to pull myself back up.

I actually have a bit of a shocking rule around burning out, because I encourage it (kids, don't try this at home!). I use it as a tactic. I burn out at least once or twice every quarter — and I do it on purpose. I think the work I do during that time is often better, especially if I'm on a roll or really finding my flow. So, I let it happen. Then I take a rest and reset.

Even the most successful people hit slumps. It's normal, but it's how you work through those moments that is key. It's when your mindset is the most important.

I know I've hit a wall when I no longer feel like doing things. I once spoke to a psychologist about it, who told me to just look at one challenge at a time instead of getting overwhelmed by all the things on my to-do list. She encouraged me to just do one thing each day, and be happy about it. Once you master just one thing, the next day you might be able to master two things. The next week, maybe you can conquer three things in a day. Tap into that momentum.

'The same way you can spiral downwards, you can spiral upwards.'

Fred Schebesta

I also highly recommend turning off all inputs when you're feeling really overwhelmed. Turn them off, and take some time out for yourself. Do something you would never normally do. My timeout is running. I never run with music and I always run alone. Some people find that time in the shower, but I find showers too intense.

Whenever I feel really burnt out, I try to remember my 'why', and I seek out the company of people who inspire me. If they're not answering, I turn inwards, and I listen to music, watch a movie or read a book. It's an attempt to reach into my head and wake up the guy who tells me to keep going; I need him to rejoin the party and reassure me that all the hard work we've been doing is moving towards the ultimate goal of building a legacy company that will outlive me.

For inspiration, my go-to movie is *Moneyball*. It depicts possibly one of the greatest examples of bringing together the most unusual group of people to make an unbeatable crew. The first time I saw this movie I was on a long-haul flight home. I cried 11 times.

If I want to pick up a book, it's usually *The 7 Habits of Highly Effective People* by Stephen Covey. This book has inspired me in a number of ways, but my biggest takeaway has been Covey's lessons on beginning with the end in mind.

I have a list of my favourite resources in each of the six steps in my online course. Head to fredschebesta.com to check it out.

MENTORS OVER METEORS

> **'With a growth mindset, kids don't necessarily think that there's no such thing as talent or that everyone is the same, but they believe everyone can develop their abilities through hard work, strategies, and lots of help and mentoring from others.'**
>
> Dr Carol Dweck

What I love about Dweck's work on the growth mindset is that she talks about the importance of mentors – of which I've had many.

Most of my mentors have come from books, videos, interviews and the many podcasts I've listened to. I've never had a lot of personal mentors. I think I have been a little intimidated to ask people to help me. But I've learnt to lean into that fear and focus on building relationships with highly successful people.

One of my first ever mentors was my ex-wife's father. His name is Michael Kiely and he was a creative director. He taught me a lot about marketing and advertising. Before he moved into marketing, Michael taught history as a lecturer at a university. I never formally studied marketing, so he was an incredible teacher to me, and he impressed upon me how to communicate a message to people.

He would take me to client pitches, I'd write copy with him, and we'd talk about concepts, about humanity, about how people feel and how they react – the fundamentals of marketing. I have been refining and mastering this for over 20 years.

Another one of my earliest mentors was Allen Olivo. Olivo is an OG of tech marketing and worked under Steve Jobs at Apple, and he has many accolades to his name. Bomber introduced us when he was in Sydney, and I remember meeting him again at a small bar in San Francisco.

He was sipping a martini at the back of the room. He told me stories about his time at Apple and the learnings from Steve Jobs – things like, 'No one cares about the bits and the bytes. People don't care what the computer can do, they care about what they can do with a computer.' That's the thing with computers, no one cares about the RAM and all the stuff that's inside a computer. A techie cares, but no one else really cares. They just care about whether they can stream Netflix or check their socials or send an email.

Olivo taught me that you need to make your message super simple, and it needs to provocatively talk to the human and not to the rational side of things. It's not about what the company wants. You need to deeply connect with the person. But to make it really simple is extraordinarily hard.

Over the past 20 years, I've spent a lot of time reading biographies and learning from great leaders and the meteor showers that they have faced. So, it works out that I have about three mentors every year. A few that stand out include *Singo*, about John Singleton by Gerald Stone; *Losing my Virginity* by Sir Richard Branson; and *The Everything Store* about Jeff Bezos by Brad Stone.

I now celebrate other people's accomplishments, and I don't feel down on myself for achieving less. I seek out people who inspire me and I want to learn from them.

MASTER YOUR INNER DIALOGUE

I had a major breakthrough when my emotional coach Craig asked me to cast my mind back to when I was teaching my daughters how to walk. He said, 'How did you speak to them when they fell down?'

I answered him honestly. I said I would coax them, hold their hands, encourage them and tell them what they were doing was really cool. Then he asked me, 'How do you speak to yourself when you fall down?' Again, I answered him honestly. I said I tell myself that I'm stupid, I'm useless, and how could I do that?

As these words were coming out of my mouth, I suddenly stopped. The penny dropped. I could be so much kinder to myself.

The next time you fail or make a mistake, try talking to yourself like you would to a child. Tell yourself that it's okay to fall down, and encourage yourself to get back up and try again.

Children are great examples of living with a growth mindset. Don't lose your inner child. Keep making mistakes.

WHAT'S THE WORST THAT COULD HAPPEN?

If you're prepared to attempt 10,000 hours to reach the elusive 'expert' status like Ericsson recommends, you're going to fail multiple times.

But the good news is this: the more you fall down, the less you worry about falling down.

Once you've screwed up something once, you realise it wasn't the end of the world. You prove to yourself that you've come back from a setback before, so you can do it again. And so, you dive in again, a little less afraid of what might happen if it doesn't go to plan.

Every problem is an opportunity for growth. Whenever I'm thinking about new ideas, I always try to identify the biggest potential problems possible. What's the worst that could happen? Once I acknowledge this, I know I would be able to deal with that worst-case scenario, which makes me confident that I'll be able to deal with smaller problems that come up too.

Ciao always says he loves mistakes because then he will know what to fix.

IT'S A 'NO' FROM ME

No. It's one of the hardest things to hear, and yet through the lens of a growth mindset, it can actually help you.

How can you be upset about something that will ultimately help you succeed?

When I first started pitching my ideas, I would cold-call people in the *Yellow Pages*. I used to hear 'no' all day. On a single call you might need to speak to several different people before you get put through to the person you're looking for.

My advice? Take the 'no' and all of the rejection, and put it in your pocket as fuel to fire yourself up and go faster. It's literally a gift.

Rejection, feedback and criticism are all going to be a part of your journey. In a lot of cases, they will help you grow. In some cases, you need to ask yourself whether that piece of criticism is constructive. If it's not, you can simply decline it.

Feedback is simply a perspective – one that you can consider, and then either act upon or decline. The real mastery is when you can be emotionally unattached from that process.

EVERY DAY I'M HUSTLIN'

Whether you're just starting out or you're at the helm of a successful business, an entrepreneurial mindset is always necessary. Because it's all about the hustle.

One of my first jobs was selling pizzas in a call centre. And I hustled hard. I became the sixth-highest upseller. I'd upsell everything. It sounded a little like: 'Hey, man, I can hear your kids in the background. Maybe we'll get them a four-pack of ice creams? It's only four bucks extra and you get a free Pepsi.' The way I suggested it to them, it seemed crazy to turn it down. They agreed almost every time.

I have always loved hustling. It's about making sure you have the best deal. It's about winning. Nothing fires me up like winning, and the small wins count just as much as the big wins!

When we secured our first office lease in New York City in 2016, I realised we needed to kit out the office space. We needed a whiteboard.

Whiteboards are funny things. Sometimes you bring them into an office and they never get used. But sometimes a whiteboard becomes the mecca for ideas in meetings.

Whiteboards were going for about US$120 online at the time. It was money I didn't want to spend on something that might only be used once. I was in startup mode, looking for every possible way to save money. So, I found a whiteboard on Craigslist for $8 and I ran across the Brooklyn Bridge to collect it. (That saved me another $40 on cabs, too.)

When you're a big company, it's just as much of a hustle, but the things you're hustling for are bigger wins and they take longer to get.

For instance, when you're looking to fill an executive role, buy a business or build bigger projects, the stakes are much higher. The Finder app took almost two years to build. We tried to hustle new features in the app such as an API connection to Up Bank. The bank released an API for its users to pull their bank transaction data, and so we added this to our app so Up Bank customers could use our app with their data. We hustled super hard to get that live before any other app.

That's the level of hustle that you need every single day.

FIND YOUR CHICKEN BURGER

Growing, challenging, changing and bettering yourself, your business and your crew can be exhausting. Sometimes, I just need a chicken burger. And sometimes, the time I spend eating a chicken burger is just as important as the time I spend hustling.

When I was younger and didn't have much cash, my luxury treat was to go and buy a chicken burger. I'd spend less than five bucks, but it was *my* five bucks. It was just something simple and it picked me up. It still does.

Stopping, sitting down and eating that burger usually gives me a few moments to do something that's not connected to work.

And sometimes, in this quiet moment, my mind wanders and works out all the stuff going on in the background of my life.

It takes me to a slightly different mental place, one where I'm suddenly able to see things differently. It's a bit like turning a painting slightly to the left, then standing in a different corner of the room and looking at it for a while.

It's my reboot. In a crazy time, I always know: hey, I can still get a chicken burger.

So, what's your chicken burger? And how are you creating space to look at a problem differently?

MY RULES FOR BUILDING A GROWTH MINDSET

1. Say YES

Saying 'yes' to things allows you to seize opportunities. You never know what growth an opportunity might bring. A chance meeting with the right person could change your entire strategy.

I've been to events I didn't want to go to and met people who turned out to be real game-changers in my career. I said 'yes' to learning new skills that I didn't think would be useful, and they ultimately were.

As an entrepreneur, you've got to say 'yes' to long hours, to hustling, to working on the fly. It's non-negotiable when you're starting out. Every spare second is time you can invest in your business.

But I also said 'yes' to myself and what I wanted to do. And that enabled me to feel *more* empowered. It gave me the space to be myself and innovate and create.

Saying 'yes' should feel uncomfortable – that's the aim here. I want to get you to an uncomfortable place, because that's where the growth happens.

2. When you feel like giving up, push on

It's always darkest right next to the spotlight. Success lies just outside of your comfort zone. It's when you feel like giving up, but instead you keep going, that you achieve remarkable things.

I have a very vivid memory of sitting next to Ciao in my car, just crying. This was in our Freestyle Media days, and we had really hit a wall. We were unsuccessful. We had been wearing the same clothes for the last 12 months, we were sleeping in the office to avoid spending the petrol money to drive home, and we'd just been hit with a quarter of a million–dollar tax bill. I remember the feeling so well. It's a physical pain that manifests in your muscles; my face was aching.

Ciao said: 'It's time to quit.'

I could understand where he was coming from. In many ways, it felt like the end of the line. We were bone-weary with exhaustion.

But I replied, 'We're not quitting. Other people can do it. We just need to find a way forward.'

And we did. It took some time, and plenty more bumps in the road, but we 'made it'.

Banksy said it best: 'Learn to rest, not to quit.'

Most of the times when I win, it's because I refuse to give up.

3. Add an extra 2 percent of effort to everything you do

This rule is about going above and beyond. It will never disadvantage you.

Effort is your path to growth and mastery. The more you put in and reach for that extra 2 percent, the better the outcome will be.

It's always when I have finished that I take a step back and think, what else can I add? That last 2 percent of effort can make a huge impact. It's where you go from being good to great.

As Malcolm Gladwell, author of *Outliers: The Story of Success* puts it, 'Success is a function of persistence and doggedness and the willingness to work hard for 22 minutes to make sense of something that most people would give up on after 30 seconds.'

'LEARN TO REST, NOT TO QUIT.'

BANKSY

4. Thank people for their feedback

Because a growth mindset requires you to be okay with rejection, failure and making mistakes, feedback is a sure-fire way to get you there.

Feedback isn't a personal attack; it is a chance to grow. Welcome feedback, appreciate it and don't take it personally. If you're thankful for it, it can't hurt you. It can only help you.

Feedback is an opportunity to gain different perspectives and insights from others. It should not be used as a way to reinforce oppressive beliefs or fears in your head. You have my permission to dismiss feedback that isn't constructive or helpful. But say 'thank you' anyway.

You might be familiar with the Finder ads on TV in Australia that have the jingle: 'finder dot com dot au!'. I've had *so much* feedback about them. I've been told they're terrible, that they're the worst. Someone said they will never visit the website again after seeing the ad.

To me, that's great feedback. The fact that someone would go out of their way to tell me they don't like the ad shows the impact it's having. Good luck getting that jingle out of your head for the rest of the day. And thanks for your feedback.

5. Celebrate successful people

When Dweck compares people with a fixed mindset versus a growth mindset, she looks at how they respond to other successful people. Someone with a fixed mindset feels threatened by the success of others. Someone with a growth mindset finds inspiration in others' success.

You will need help getting to the top, whether it be from your peers, competitors or mentors. So, the same way you expect your support network to cheer for your wins, cheer for theirs too.

PRINCIPLE 3

Do things that have meaning to you

'He who has a why can endure any how.'

FRIEDRICH NIETZSCHE

IT'S USUALLY AN IDEA THAT WAKES ME UP like a bolt of lightning.

I don't really have a regular routine, but I usually wake up around 1am. The first thing I do is pick up a notebook and pen from my bedside and write down ideas, reflections and goals.

I open my emails, respond to messages and read over reports and contracts that have come through from the different Finder offices across the world.

I spend a few hours here, and then go back to sleep for an hour or two. I'm up again at about 6am before my first round of meetings for the day, starting at 7am.

After the morning meetings, it's time to get fired up for the day ahead. I put on my favourite rap playlist (I have one I made on Spotify called 'Rap Billions'). Then I hit the beach for a 10km run. I do some of my best thinking while running. I love the peace and serenity of being alone. It's when I can rearrange my thoughts.

After taking my daughters to school, I drive to the office while listening to a podcast or taking some calls. Then I'll grab a take-away large soy latte and some smashed avocado on toast, and I'm plugged into my computer at my standing desk by 10am.

A routine like this might not be for you. But I'm here to tell you, if you're not fired up on Monday mornings, then you're in the wrong job.

I'm excited by every day of the week. The first thoughts that usually run through my head are: what am I going to create today? What wormhole am I going to go down? How can we do what we're doing already but better? That's because I've found my purpose.

> **'My purpose is to challenge and inspire people to achieve unimaginable success.'**
>
> Fred Schebesta

I want to reach hyper success. I want to build a legacy that outlives me. I want to create a business that continues to better people's lives for the next 100 years – and beyond.

Hyper success is about reaching the highest possible level of achievement in every way: mentally, physically and spiritually. I want to *win*. It's about living the absolute best I can and sharing my learnings with others to help them achieve their own success.

My goal is to make Finder the Amazon of comparison.

One day, Finder will be able to do your banking for you. It will save you money before you even know there's money to be saved. I want to help the underbanked, raise the poverty line and increase financial literacy. And I'll wake up at 1am every single day to move my mission forward, if that's what it takes.

Knowing *why* I do things is very different to knowing *how* I do them. The reason why I do what I do helps me to keep going. It motivates me when I'm burning the candle at both ends, it inspires me when I'm faced with a difficult decision, and it's the little voice cheering me on when I'm tired and want to quit.

And that 'why' will always be relevant, because even once you reach a certain level of success, things aren't going to suddenly get easier. In fact, they will probably get harder. The stakes will be higher, so doing things that have meaning to you will be even more important. That is why Principle 3 is to do things that have meaning to you.

So, why do you do what you do? And how will that impact the purpose of your business?

WHY IS 'WHY' IMPORTANT?

Author Simon Sinek first popularised the concept of knowing your 'why' in a TED talk back in 2009. Today, the video has been watched by over 54 million people.

In the talk, Sinek explains why every business and leader should 'start with why' in mind. Because why you're doing what you're doing will be the reason customers choose your product, why they'll come to you.

For example, Sinek looks at why a company like Apple has had so much success. It's just a tech company, right? Wrong. Apple sets itself apart from its competitors because it operates from a place of *purpose*.

Sinek compares two possible Apple marketing strategies:

'We make great computers. They're beautifully designed, simple to use and user friendly. Want to buy one?'

Versus:

'Everything we do, we believe in challenging the status quo. We believe in thinking differently. The way we challenge the status quo is by making our products beautifully designed, simple to use and user friendly. We just happen to make great computers. Want to buy one?'

Which computer are you going to buy?

While most companies know *what* they do, and *how* they do it, fewer know 'why' they do what they do. Olivo told me about Sinek's 'Golden Circle', which explains why successful companies like Apple lead with the 'why' – and there's actually a neurological scientific principle behind it.

'People don't buy what you do, they buy why you do it.'

SIMON SINEK

Sinek compares the Golden Circle to the human brain. The 'WHAT' is our neocortex – the part of the brain responsible for rational thought. The 'HOW' and 'WHY' circles are the limbic parts of the brain. They are responsible for our feelings and decision-making.

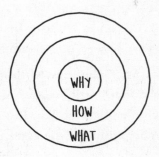

When companies market themselves from a place of 'WHAT', they are appealing to the rational part of our brains, whereas when they connect with the customer from a place of 'WHY' they appeal directly to the emotional and decision-making parts.

In Sinek's words, 'People don't buy what you do, they buy why you do it.'

IT'S OKAY TO GO LIVE BEFORE YOU HAVE FOUND YOUR PURPOSE

When Ciao and I started Finder, we were lucky to have a solid purpose from the beginning. Finder has always been about helping people live a better life. We believe in empowering people with the right tools and education to make better decisions and save money.

We knew what we wanted to do. We knew how we were going to start. And we knew why we were doing it.

But not all businesses start out like this, and I believe that it's okay to launch a business without your purpose precisely laid out from the very beginning.

When we consider Apple, Steve Jobs humanised the computer and made it feel like more than a computer to many people. He made the humble mobile phone a can't-live-without extra limb. As humans, we love to attach meaning to things, and having no meaning can make us feel uncomfortable.

Whether Jobs intended to do things this way or not, I submit to you that you can start a business without being 100 percent clear on your 'why'. But you will need one eventually.

So, whether you're starting a business without a purpose or you have the 'why' first, it doesn't really matter in what order you Go Live, because your 'why' will come. You just need to start with a goal. But you should start putting some conscious thought towards your purpose. Really hard questions and problems take time.

HERE'S HOW TO WORK OUT *YOUR* WHY

According to Sinek, a 'why' is a cause, a belief and a reason that your organisation exists.

So, putting your business idea aside for a minute, think about this: in your day-to-day life, what are your true underlying motivations?

If you look at how you carry out each day, your 'why' underpins everything you do. You make healthy choices because you want to live long enough to meet your great-grandchildren; you refinance your mortgage because you want to save for a holiday; you read that book because you want to be a better manager.

Humans are hardwired for purpose. But sometimes it takes a little probing to get to the real reason that we do most things. Here's an example:

Q: Why do you go to the gym?

A: Because I want to lose weight.

Q. Why do you want to lose weight?

A: Because I want to fit into my old clothes.

Q: Why do you want to fit into your old clothes?

A: Because they make me feel more confident.

Q: Why do you want to feel more confident?

A: Because if I have more confidence, I won't be scared to present that award, or go swimming at the beach, or ask for a promotion, or go on that date. I'll be able to do all the things I am scared to do.

There's your why!

I challenge you to ask yourself why you do most of the things you do. And keep asking why until you get to the root of the reason.

Once you've had a good think about why *you* do certain things, start asking the same questions of your business idea. What is its purpose in the world? What is it here to do for other people? How is it contributing to making the planet better?

REAL TALK: MONEY ISN'T THE ONLY 'WHY'

I have a confession. When I first started out in business, my first mission was to make $1 million. Deep down it was because I wanted to prove my parents wrong. I wanted to make more money than they had and be more successful than they were. I wanted to prove to them that I could make something of myself without conforming to what everyone expected. I wanted to do things differently.

I thought this million-dollar goal was my purpose. But over the years, I realised that money isn't a purpose.

Sinek agrees. He says, to make a profit *is* a direct result of your 'why', but it *isn't* your 'why'.

The reason money isn't your purpose is because there's probably not going to be much of it in the initial stages of starting a business. And you need something you deeply connect to, to keep you motivated and committed when you're working 100 hours a week and investing your all into an idea that has no guarantee of success – and might not ever pay off.

I have so many memories of living in my first share house with Ciao in the early days, like when I used to watch just one DVD on repeat: *Wall Street*. This was before Netflix, when we had to go to Blockbuster to rent movies. I would watch this one DVD over and over again, simply because that DVD was the only one I had. I couldn't afford to hire movies. I had no money to go out.

I kept going because I had a goal, which eventually turned into my purpose. Back then, all that kept my belly full was a desire to succeed. That was all I needed – the determination to never give up.

Money will never be a barometer of success, because at what point have you made enough to deem your business venture successful? $1 million? $5 million? $50 million? $500 million?

There's always more money to be made, and you could spend the rest of your life striving for an unattainable goal. The game is infinite.

Nowadays, the money I make is simply a bonus. The real happiness for me comes from knowing Finder is helping people make better choices and live better lives, and the company is well on its way to outlive me.

MY 'WHY'

My purpose has changed a lot over the years. I started with a monetary goal, I achieved it and then I asked myself: what's next? There's no prize for having the greatest purpose. You have to keep evolving your 'why' as you go.

My personal motivation isn't money, power or control. It's actually the opposite. In one word, my 'why' is freedom.

'THE GAME IS INFINITE.'

FRED SCHEBESTA

At Finder, we've created a product that frees people. Our product gives people the freedom to make better financial decisions. And in return, I am also free. I have freedom.

Most people who want to take the entrepreneurial path have a similar motivation. They crave freedom in some capacity – whether that's financial freedom, creative freedom or the freedom to do something in their own way.

I realised this at a time when I wasn't feeling very free. It was 2015 and I was in a really dark place. I had this image stuck inside my head: it was of me sitting on a chair in the middle of a dark room. It was completely black – there were no windows, just a door. And as I was sitting there, I could see the door start to close.

This dark time for me culminated in the year that I was finalising my divorce. Like a lot of people who go through big life adjustments, I was a little off the rails... maybe a lot.

I receded to a place in the company where I basically had no direct reports. I was handing over responsibility to avoid wreaking havoc. When I look back on that time, I basically got fired. I wasn't forcibly removed, but I was disappearing into the background.

My adrenal glands were working overtime and I was constantly on edge. Everything was heightened. Everything was a big deal. Everything was loud, and I was so sensitive to it. I was on high alert. It didn't feel healthy, and I wasn't in a place where I could keep operating at the level I wanted to be at. I was a fighter jet pilot who had to hand over the keys for a while.

I called a meeting with Ciao. We met at a cafe, and I said to him: 'I'm not sure what I do here anymore.'

Ciao suggested that I stay at my desk and people will come to me for help. So, I did this for a while and worked on some small projects. But after some time had passed, we both realised that wasn't working.

I approached him again and I suggested, 'What if I go overseas and start the US business?'

Ciao agreed. My divorce was finalised and I was ready for a new beginning. I was off on my next adventure. In a matter of weeks, I found myself on a plane with a huge challenge ahead of me. I had a new purpose and I felt invincible.

Taking that leap didn't come without its challenges. The week before I left, I had a physical reaction to my anxiety: I broke out in a full-body rash. It had happened to me once before, when Ciao and I first sold Freestyle Media, so I knew what it was: it was literally my fears and anxieties manifesting on the outside of my body.

I would scratch my skin until it bled, and stand underneath scalding hot water in the shower to feel some relief. I applied creams and tried everything to deal with it, but it didn't go away... until I touched down in Manhattan. As soon as I landed my rash was gone. I was alive again. New York City brought me back to life.

ESCAPING MY LIFE TO FIND MYSELF

Leaving Sydney for New York City was a huge turning point for me. The experience and discomfort made me turn inward, and I started some deep introspection. I figured out who I was and what I love to do.

I love to create. I love to build things. I love to be given the freedom to do those things, and I love creating safe places for other people to do the same.

In New York, this is when I started to find my own purpose.

I don't regret any of the time I spent soul-searching during that year. I learnt a great deal about myself, and I made a lot of mistakes that I'm proud to say I have grown from. I think that, as humans, our lives will always ebb and flow. I believe we're either motivated by pleasure or pain.

You either love to win or you hate to lose. That pain motivated me. It made me really hungry and excited about what I could sink my teeth into next. It was the pain I needed to grow and move on to the next chapter in my journey.

Taking Finder to the US gave me that freedom to create something new – to build something from the ground up. I remember taking Bomber for a look around our first New York City office space in 2016. I gave him a tour, and he sat in on one of our weekly UTTR meetings (it stands for Up and To The Right, like the direction you want the line to go in a graph) – the same meetings we have in our Australian office.

Afterwards, he pulled me aside. Bomber's words hit me to my core and I started to cry. He said, 'Man, you've done it again. You've created Finder in another country. We're on the other side of the world, and it still feels like Finder!'

That was a real lightbulb moment for me in finding my 'why'. I take things from zero to 100. And I realised I'm actually pretty good at it.

Pay attention to what you naturally gravitate towards. What are the things, challenges, conversations that make you tick? What feels like it's raising your vibrations? What work doesn't feel like work to you? When you identify these moments, it means you're getting closer to your purpose.

MEMENTO MORI

I have a monthly reminder in my calendar. It goes off on the seventh day of every month and it says, 'Memento Mori', which directly translates to 'remember that you die'.

I first came across the concept of memento mori when I was watching a video of Steve Jobs on YouTube. He was giving a commencement address at the University of Stanford back in 2005.

He said:

> 'Remembering that I'll be dead soon is the most important
> tool I've ever encountered to help me make the big choices
> in life. Because almost everything – all external expectations,
> all pride, all fear of embarrassment or failure – these things
> just fall away in the face of death, leaving only what is truly
> important. Remembering that you are going to die is the
> best way I know to avoid the trap of thinking you have
> something to lose. You are already naked.'

I have learnt a lot from Jobs. He was a great storyteller, and these
words particularly resonated with me. When I first saw his commencement speech, I ended up in one of those internet spirals
where you just keep exploring something, and clicking through
to the next relevant thing, and then the next thing – I am a sucker
for clickbait!

So I was in deep, researching the concept of memento mori after
watching the video of Jobs, and I found myself on this random site
with a whole series of photographs of people taken right before
they died.

There was a photo of Paul Walker from the movie *The Fast and the
Furious*; he was just standing there in front of his car, not knowing
this would be the last photo ever taken of him – and I just couldn't
stop looking at it. Another was of Heath Ledger on the set of
his last film, *The Imaginarium of Doctor Parnassus*. I was transfixed.
And scared.

At that point I think the finality of life and death really dawned on
me, and ever since then I've considered it a key motivator. I want
to do a lot before I get to the end. It motivates me to do it right
now, do it today, get it done. I re-ground myself with memento
mori on a regular basis.

BEGIN WITH THE END IN MIND

Earlier I mentioned one of my favourite books: *The 7 Habits of Highly Effective People,* by Stephen Covey. In it, Covey talks about this idea of 'beginning with the end in mind', which is extremely useful when trying to work out your purpose for doing what you're doing, and is a similar concept to memento mori.

In the book, Covey encourages readers to imagine their own funeral. He creates the entire scene in the reader's mind: the coffin, the flowers, even the soft organ music. The reader takes a seat inside the church, and then Covey asks them: what would you like each of the speakers to say about your life?

To begin with the end in mind 'is to begin today with the image, picture or paradigm of the end of your life as your frame of reference or the criterion by which everything else is examined'.

The same goes for you and your business. In your wildest dreams, what is the legacy you want to create? And how are you working towards that?

Your business idea should be in line with your values. It should be something you believe in and something you are proud to dedicate your life to.

'It's incredibly easy to get caught up in the activity trap, in the busy-ness of life, to work harder and harder at climbing the ladder of success only to discover it's leaning against the wrong wall... We may be very busy, we may be very efficient, but we will also be truly effective only when we begin with the end in mind.'

Stephen Covey

Let yourself dream about just how epic this business idea of yours could be, and imagine me at your funeral saying you were the most rockstar founder I ever knew.

MAKE IT A MISSION

Knowing your own 'why' is going to seep into why you're embarking on this business journey, and will most likely help you define your purpose in business.

But figuring out your company's 'why' is one step. The next is to make a daily commitment to it.

The purpose of and reason for your business idea needs to underpin and permeate through every corner of operations in your company. That's why I believe a mission statement is so important.

A mission statement puts you and your team on the same page. It gives every crew member and contractor a clear understanding of how their work will contribute to the overall success of the business.

Check out these mission statements from game-changing companies across the world. Just like Sinek's Apple comparison, can you see how these statements clearly show their 'why', not their 'what'?

- 'We ignite opportunity by setting the world in motion.'
  – Uber
- 'Fill the world with emotion, through the power of creativity and technology.' – Sony
- 'Give people the power to build community and bring the world closer together.' – Facebook
- 'To inspire and nurture the human spirit – one person, one cup, and one neighborhood at a time.' – Starbucks
- 'We want to entertain the world.' – Netflix
- 'Our mission is to make delicious feel-good moments easy for everyone.' – McDonald's

At Finder, our mission is, 'To better all the world's decisions.' I think we're lucky that our mission and purpose and what we do are so closely aligned. It means they aren't just words plastered on a wall. Our purpose is part of our lexicon. It's in the language we use every day. It is the reason we do everything we do.

If you don't know why you're doing what you do, or it doesn't mean anything to you, or if it's not fun too many times in a row, change it.

Years ago, my partner Brenda was wrangling with choosing her purpose. She kept going in mental circles and was totally stuck.

I said to her, 'Seriously, it doesn't matter, just pick one. Pick a purpose that feels right to you and start with that. If it's not right, you can change it. The beauty of a purpose is you get to pick what it is, and it's never fixed in place.'

Brenda was consuming so much energy trying to figure out this mega-super-important purpose, and she kept feeling like she was coming up short. There was also this underlying pressure – the idea that once she decided on her purpose, it was locked in forever.

In reality, things change constantly. We evolve every day. And there is a lot of value in just picking something, even if it isn't some grand idea that could change the world.

You'll pivot and adapt, and your purpose will evolve with you. So, don't get stuck on this premise, and instead enjoy the process of testing what that purpose is and what it means to you compared to alternatives.

Life is too short to live with regrets. Start by doing something that's worth doing and you'll build a company with people who share the same purpose.

PRINCIPLE 4

Be the ultimate creative expression of yourself

'No one is you and that is your biggest power.'

DAVE GROHL

DURING A JOB INTERVIEW, one of the first things I ask a potential candidate is, 'What is your superpower? What are you 100 times better at than everyone else?'

Their answer is key, because I believe in focusing on strengths. Principle 4 is to be the ultimate creative expression of yourself, and you can only do this by knowing what you're really, truly good at. Being the ultimate creative expression of yourself is about living your superpower.

I think everyone has what I call 'geniuses', which are what they are naturally exceptional at. Take Roger Federer. The Swiss tennis player has kinetic genius. In other words, he knows how to kinetically use his body to win tennis matches against the best players in the world.

Some people have interpersonal genius, and they know how to influence people; they know what words to use in conversation and how to hold a room. Others have mathematical genius, or exceptional empathy. Some people are visionaries, artists or great with words.

What is it that you naturally gravitate towards when you start a project? What's the first thing you do? Whatever it is, there is probably some clue in there as to your genius. And that's what you want to focus on.

Public service announcement: now is not the time to try to improve your accounting skills if you've spent your whole life outsourcing your taxes because you don't like numbers and you're terrible at it. Now is the time to truly capitalise on what makes you better than everyone else. This is the core of Principle 4.

At this point in time, you're probably the greatest asset inside your business — even if you are the only asset!

WHEN I FOUND MY SUPERPOWER

I found my superpower when I was at Macquarie University in 1999.

I was studying actuarial studies and computer science, but neither really made me tick. I wasn't having fun. And I was failing. Before long, I tapped out and stopped going to my classes.

I was there doing what everyone expected me to do: following the traditional path and using a university degree to hopefully land a great job. But I felt lost, and I started to lose confidence in myself.

I was living a double life. University wasn't a happy place for me, but building websites in my spare time was where I found true joy. My love affair with the internet was conceived in my dorm room on a cold, lonely night in July. This was before hashtags and WordPress — people literally had to roll their own websites. It took months to code one site. And I was out there doing just that. I found myself in a pure flow state.

Computers are unbelievably powerful, and I haven't stopped being blown away by their potential. I remember during one of my projects in computer science class, we were given a bunch of numbers to sort from highest to lowest. I started writing out formulas for each step, and I found it really difficult.

My friend made the suggestion, 'Hey, why don't you just get all the numbers and compare them against each other on a computer?' My first thought was, 'That's a lot of computation and it's going to take a lot of time.' But I chucked the numbers into the computer and the answer came up immediately. Another lightbulb moment.

'Computers can do things in an instant that humans will never be able to do in their lifetime.'

Fred Schebesta

What I loved most about building websites was that I was literally creating something out of nothing. There was a moment in one of my classes when I realised how much I loved this initial creation stage. I was working on a project for one of my university subjects. It was a group project, and as a team we had to design a system. I organised everyone into roles and I established the priorities. Once everyone was on target, I got bored and didn't participate very much.

But that's my superpower: making something from nothing. Getting started. Definitely not the ongoing organisational stuff.

I made the difficult decision to quit my degree and change courses. It was one of the hardest, scariest and yet most empowering decisions of my life.

Go to where your energy flows, the things you naturally gravitate towards. That's what I did. When you are in that place – the energy zone – you are aligned. That's where my attention went; the energy flowed there, and it manifested into successful businesses.

Every year I choose a word to describe my year ahead – the one thing I want to focus on. In 2019, my word was 'energy'. I manifested this into a physical space in the office where good energy flowed.

Letting my superpower lead the way suddenly meant all of these doors started opening up for me. I could finally see a future for myself. I found a course I was interested in – Bachelor of

'GO TO WHERE YOUR ENERGY FLOWS.'

FRED SCHEBESTA

Commerce majoring in finance – and I started building websites for more people. I was rebuilding myself from the ground up.

Finding my strengths and playing to them was a key factor in my success, and that's why identifying yours is so important.

STRENGTHS OVER WEAKNESSES

When you go for a job interview, you'll often get asked about your weaknesses, but I like to focus on strengths. Your strength is the sweet spot; it's where the magic happens.

This is the area where you're going to enjoy working the most, and it's where you'll have a competitive edge that no one else will have. If you're thinking of starting a business, this is the best place to begin, because in the early days of starting a business you're going to have so much to learn – why add even more to that list?

Thinking this way in business is a relatively new thing. Positive – or 'strength-based' – psychology is something that became popular in the 1990s thanks to psychologist Donald Clifton, who asked, 'What would happen if we studied what was *right* with people versus what's *wrong* with people?'

Clifton created the CliftonStrengths (formerly Clifton Strengths-Finder) as a result of that question: a book and online assessment resource to encourage people to tap into what they're already really good at. We've used it with the crew at Finder.

CliftonStrengths helps people identify where they are unique and powerful. Research by global analytics and advisory firm Gallup has shown that those who know and play to their strengths every day are:

- three times more likely to report excellent quality of life
- six times more likely to be engaged at work
- 8 percent more productive
- 15 percent less likely to quit their jobs.

I can personally attest to these statistics. I am someone who always plays to my strengths, and I find other people to help me in the areas where I'm not as strong.

CliftonStrengths categorises strength in 34 different themes across four different key domains: executing, influencing, relationship building and strategic thinking.

The executing types are practical and motivated; they are the 'doers' and won't stop until they've successfully achieved their goal. The influential types are – no surprises – influencers; they create momentum and are usually good communicators. The relationship-building types use human connection to achieve results and are usually what is referred to as the 'glue' of the team. The strategic-thinking types drive ideas and forward-think with a laser focus. That last one is me!

You can do the CliftonStrengths assessment online for a small investment; it's less than $100, and you gain a whole stack of insights that can help you find clarity about where you really need to focus.

Knowing what you do better than anyone else and focusing on this strength is your superpower. It's going to propel you further ahead than your competitors and give you an edge that others don't have; so, in these early planning stages, take some time to get introspective.

WHEN IT'S TIME TO FIRE YOURSELF

I have done a lot of introspective work, and I'm the first to admit where both my strengths and weaknesses lie. You literally can't have one without the other, so it's crucial to be clear on both ends.

I know I am good at vision, focus, strategy, ideation and creativity. And I know I need help in management, planning and sometimes communication.

While I think it's important to play to your strengths, it's equally important to recognise if, and when, your weaknesses become a limiting factor in your company's overall success. You need to be aware of your weaknesses, because if you can't deal emotionally with where the company needs to go, then you'll be actively (if not willingly) sabotaging your company's success.

If you're too scared to go out and try things, your blocks will become the company's blocks. So, know when it's time to put your hand up for help.

I have been the blocker of my own company's growth before. About six years ago, I wasn't emotionally prepared enough to deal with some big adjustments in my life, and Finder was growing faster than I was. It was around the time when my divorce was being finalised and I found myself alone.

I started to become destructive to everyone around me. I wouldn't show up to meetings, and I would engage in conflicts with people. I kept making the same mistakes over and over again, and I finally admitted the problem was beyond me. I needed outside help; I didn't know how to deal with the fears and issues that were boiling over. I was out of control.

I've been doing some hard work on myself ever since, with the help of my emotional coach, Craig. I pulled myself through my rut and came out the other side as a better person. It took me a while to learn that I am one of my own best assets. You need to look after yourself and invest in your personal development, otherwise you might pull down everyone around you.

After the first few sessions with my emotional coach, I pulled my co-founders aside and I said, 'I want to apologise because I have been the limiting factor for this entire company. I am committed to changing that and improving myself.'

It was a very emotional meeting, and I am grateful to have had Bomber and Ciao's support while I was going through a rough

'YOUR STRENGTH IS THE SWEET SPOT; IT'S WHERE THE MAGIC HAPPENS.'

FRED SCHEBESTA

time. They gave me the space I needed to find my feet, and they helped me find my purpose, which led to us expanding Finder into the US and over 70 other countries.

There are two lessons you can take away from this: first and foremost, ask for help when you need it. Secondly, hire the people who can do the things that you're not great at.

THERE IS NO BATMAN WITHOUT ROBIN

After setting up the US office and getting the team established, I was ready to move back to Australia. Once I got home from New York, I was much clearer on the unique skills I brought to the company. It wasn't the operating part. I was the originator. The creator. And at that time, I was able to get really clear with Ciao about our roles.

Ciao took on the operations. I knew I wasn't as good at that. While you don't have to find a business partner (there are plenty of people who have found great success on their own), I knew I needed one.

I have known Ciao for a very long time. We met at high school when we were 13 years old. We were in the same grade, and one of the first things I remember about him was that he was really funny. He was a bit different, and he was naturally gifted on the sports field.

We became close friends by Year 10. We'd go out together to parties and get up to mischief the way typical 16-year-olds do. We studied at different universities, but we stayed in touch. After uni finished, we started living together with some friends in a share house. That's where we came up with our first business, Freestyle Media.

Where I am very marketing and product-based, Ciao's strengths are in operations and finance. I'm the visionary who is always looking ahead at which direction we need to take, and Ciao sees it through. Ciao is an incredible leader and we have a yin-and-yang dynamic. Our skills complement each other. We call it follower-ship at Finder, where sometimes it's really powerful and equally important to choose to follow someone and support them in lead-ing. Other times it's your turn to step up.

Ciao and I have been running businesses together for about 20 years – that's longer than most marriages! It's the ideal partnership. If he is the stable building, I am the electricity running through it.

Back in 2016, I made a speech at Ciao's wedding and I told the congregation, 'There is no Fred without Frank.' Ciao complements and completes all of my weaknesses, and all of the elements and blind spots I have to make me whole.

The reason Ciao and I work so well together is because we have the same values but different strengths. Before we agreed to start working together, we spent one afternoon writing down our values on separate pieces of paper. When we were done, we compared them. They were nearly identical!

One of those values was 'legacy'. That has always stayed with me because I knew that we were on the same page with what we wanted to achieve: a legacy business for the world and for our families. A business that will outlive all of us.

Values are so important because you and your business partner will not agree on every micro detail, but if you have the same big-picture values, there is a good chance you'll agree on the big stuff. And that's what matters most.

While Ciao naturally took the role of CEO, I filled the role of Chief Creative Officer. There are some blurred lines between a CEO and a CCO, and both mainly co-exist in the early stages of a new company.

Hugh Hefner is a great example of a Chief Creative Officer. He had a real hand in the experience of *Playboy*, and was a frontward-facing product of the brand. He was a visionary. That's my superpower.

You might not need a CEO or a business partner, and that's for you to decide. You might consider yourself well-rounded enough and have all the dimensions already covered. You might also prefer to go down the path of engaging advisors and directors for extra support. We also have advisors who help us level up.

If you're keen to find a business partner who complements your strengths and weaknesses, I recommend buying a notepad and, if you can, booking yourself into a cabin somewhere in the wilderness. At the minimum, block out a few hours and sit in a quiet room where you can really tune out the rest of the world.

Turn inwards and take some time to have a little self-assessment. Here are my tips for finding a business partner:

- Write down your strengths and weaknesses: you want to look for someone who has the exact *opposite* skills to you.
- Look ahead: what will their role be? One of you is probably going to be the CEO.
- Put them through the Monopoly test: Ciao and I have probably played 100 games of Monopoly over the years. Monopoly brings out the worst in people, and it can be such a long game. You'll quickly discover if this is someone you could do business with!
- Don't rush in: just like you wouldn't marry someone without dating them and getting to know them first, don't rush into things with a business partner.

THE AVENGERS

Business partner or no business partner, as you're gearing up to launch a business, you want to surround yourself with the right people – those who complement *your* superpower. You want to build an Avengers team.

Whenever I'm taking a metaphorical rocket ship into space, my priority is making sure we have all the astronauts with the right skills on the ship. We need someone to steer the ship, someone to navigate and someone to land. They're all equally important and valuable team members, because if one is missing, we will never complete the mission.

I personally hired at least the first 50 people at Finder in Australia, and then the first 25 in the US. I think it's absolutely critical a company founder or CEO understands the benchmark of people they want to surround themselves with. No one else will. The buck stops with you.

I'm thankful that I have solid self-awareness and awareness of other people and their skills, and I can see the potential in people. I like to put people into roles where they're having fun and are enjoying what they are doing.

Every day when I walk into the office, I look around at the people I have in certain roles and I think to myself: would I rehire this person for this role? If not, it might be because they are suited to a different role.

Justin Toladro is a Product Lead at Finder and, like everyone in the crew, has created some of the most incredible projects. But he didn't start out in the Product team. JT is one of the OGs at Finder. He began as a Graduate Publisher 10 years ago. When he first started, JT was working with me on launching Life Insurance Finder, and our small team was all working on every part of the business. JT was very results-driven.

After shifting his focus to public relations for about six months, I noticed that JT naturally led the project management and strategy work of PR campaigns. JT's superpower shone through when he moved into Product Management. This was his superpower.

JT asked me: 'What do I need to do to get to the next level? What's the next unlock?' These are the types of people I want to work with. They're self-aware, results-driven and ambitious.

There are so many people at Finder just like JT, who have started out in one role and have evolved into different roles where they are living out their full potential. They are passionate about what they do and that creates a powerful energy. There are far too many people to call them all out individually, but I'm so honoured to work with 500 incredible people every day.

IT'S ALL ABOUT ATTITUDE

It is possible to teach skills, but it's not possible to teach attitude.

Sometimes I like to work with people who don't necessarily have the skills yet but who do have the drive, passion and persistence to get big results. These people are going to get it done no matter what – their skills will develop and they will go on to master their craft, because they have the motivation to make it happen.

> **'Great companies don't hire skilled people and motivate them, they hire already motivated people and inspire them.'**
>
> Simon Sinek

One of the key qualities I look for when I'm hiring is grit. It's not a skill, it's more a question of: can you handle hard knocks? Can you handle some fast chopping and pivoting, adjusting and adapting? Because that's how I operate.

I also want to find those people who aspire to greatness. I look for the future potential of who these people will become. I don't look at who someone is today, I look at the person that they could be.

That person needs to have a bigger vision of themselves – the belief that right now, we are simply in a moment in time, a version of ourselves that can be improved every day.

I have made a conscious decision to set up Finder in this way. I want the company to be bigger than all of us, so that when it requires change or growth, we as a team are there to facilitate it. The people on my team need to know the path sometimes isn't clear; the water isn't always calm. Because you don't become a sailor on smooth seas.

WORKING OUT YOUR UNIQUE SELLING POINT (USP)

In business, your superpower may feed into your unique selling point (USP).

As we move further along this journey, this is something I'm going to encourage you to think about: what is your business's unique selling point? What is the thing that makes your business unique?

You may be selling cleaning services like a whole lot of other people, but maybe you have a special technique. Maybe you're able to reduce costs better than anyone else. Maybe you have a unique, proprietary chemical no one else uses, or your systems mean you can get the job done in half the time of your competitors.

At Finder, our USP is going deeper than anyone else. As a company, we review and compare more products, and our app has more innovative features, unlike anything else in the world.

What is it that's going to help you compete? What is it that's going to encourage customers to come to you? What will make you win?

WHAT ARE YOUR STRENGTHS AND WEAKNESSES?

Here's a hack I use to discover my superpowers. Get a journal and divide the page into two columns. Write down your strengths in one column and your weaknesses in the other, and identify the areas you might need help with along your journey.

Your superpower is where you want to start. Everything good that happens will come from there. Knowing what you're good at, and what you're not so crash hot at, will put you leaps and bounds ahead of your competitors — both on a personal and a business level.

To know your superpower is to follow this path in a way that only you can, and to know your weaknesses is to surround yourself with the best possible people to take with you along the journey. That is how you get to the next level.

PRINCIPLE 5

Manufacture serendipity

⚡

'The first step is to establish that something
is possible, then probability will occur.'

ELON MUSK

IN 2003, a friend of mine shared this quote with me: 'Early to bed. Early to rise. Work like hell and advertise.'

At the time, I don't think my friend realised what he was saying, because it really affected me in a profound way. I love this quote, from billionaire entrepreneur Ted Turner, because it says everything about what you need to do in a great company when you have a great model and a great strategy.

Ted Turner is hands-down one of the most successful entrepreneurs of our time. He founded CNN, the first 24-hour cable news channel, in 1979. As well as being the largest landowner in the US until 2011 – he owns 2 million acres of land! – and owning many other business ventures and philanthropic initiatives, Ted was a futurist, revolutionising the news media industry and capturing a market for over 40 years.

This quote meant so much to me. In fact, I still use this mantra almost 20 years later.

It's funny how something so small and almost nonchalant can have such a deep impact on your life. I call these moments 'manufactured serendipity', and this is my Principle 5.

Serendipity means a fortunate occurrence by chance – something that's out of your control. But manufactured serendipity is about connecting the random dots that you didn't realise were connected. It's about exploring the universe, seeing what possibilities will come, and the opportunities that come your way that you didn't realise were possible.

> **'Manufactured serendipity is about connecting the random dots
> that you didn't realise were connected.'**

Fred Schebesta

You can manufacture your serendipity and forge your own path. But this can only happen if you take advantage of opportunities that come your way.

This principle is all about how you can manufacture serendipity. It's about your journey of discovery. When you start to strategise your business idea, it becomes real. Your business idea will identify with an industry, you'll uncover whether there's a gap in the market for your idea and you'll start to find out who your customers are.

It's wild. You're driving a ship in unknown waters without any lights or sensors or navigation switched on. You're unsure which direction to steer in, when the seas will get choppy, if you're heading straight towards a storm or about to hit an iceberg. The only thing you can do is sit back, enjoy the ride and be prepared to change course.

THE WILD WILD WEST OF HIVEEX

When I'm looking into a new business idea, I'm usually playing to my strengths – I'm looking for industries that I already know, or that I have a connection with. But this wasn't the case for our cryptocurrency brokerage, HiveEx. It was a totally new industry for me and one of the biggest and sharpest learning curves in my career.

I'm also looking for products and services that make money. I want to know there's money in or around the industry, because that means it will probably have a greater chance of success.

Once I identify that industry, product or service, I'm going in for a deep dive. Typically I'm looking for bumps or roadblocks that

I might be able to fix. I'm looking for edge cases – customers who are on the periphery of the target and might need the product or service adjusted to them.

I'm also keeping my eyes open for those industries that need to be completely overhauled – that are so archaic and fundamentally flawed in the 21st century that they are screaming out for a saviour. This is how I felt about the crypto space.

I first heard about Bitcoin in 2009 when I was using my computer to contribute to the 'SETI project' – a distributed computer system that helps scan the universe for life. I was hanging out with my cousin Dave Coleman, who taught me how to use my computer to start 'mining' this coin called Bitcoin. But I was an amateur – I didn't really understand how it worked, and to this day I still don't know where those Bitcoins are.

I didn't have much to do with cryptocurrency again until 2017, when Bomber came to me and told me it was flying! He showed me the data, the Google trends and the lack of competition in the space. I loved the idea of working with crypto because it was a combination of my three favourite things: finance, marketing and tech. That and the fact that it was growing sparked my interest.

In January of that year, the cost of one Bitcoin was $US952. In May it was worth more than US$2000 and it kept climbing – by December 2017, one Bitcoin would set you back nearly US$20,000.

During the 2017 crypto boom, I researched the industry to work out what needed to be fixed, and found the bump: I couldn't figure out how to trade large amounts of crypto in a simple and cost-effective way. Other people started approaching me with the same problem. It was a hot topic and something I wanted to solve.

Digital currency exchanges already existed, but they were only good for trades of up to about $20,000. If you wanted to buy

'EARLY TO BED.
EARLY TO RISE.
WORK LIKE HELL
AND ADVERTISE.'

TED TURNER

or sell crypto above this, the order was usually split into smaller amounts, and each order would go up in price. This was a result of something called slippage, where each trade on an exchange means paying slightly more, due to the limited number of people selling at different prices. This meant larger trades cost up to 5 or even 10 percent more.

I discovered that the best option for doing larger trades was to use an 'over-the-counter' (OTC) brokerage or trading desk. But there weren't many options available – especially in Australia.

I'd found the wormhole, and HiveEx – a brokerage service for large 'block' volume crypto trades – was born. We were filling a gap in the market.

Unlike the brokerages already on the market, HiveEx was a trustworthy and well-lit space on the internet. I used to call crypto-currency the Wild Wild West of the internet, because it was just like when the internet was starting to take off in the late 1990s: it wasn't clear what was legit and what was a scam. You didn't know who to trust. I wanted to make HiveEx a trustworthy and safe place to trade.

Starting HiveEx came with a cast of new challenges. I had to get my head around the complexities of blockchain and digital currencies, compliance and regulation across the world, and all of the challenges the industry faced.

I noticed banks were blocking blockchain-related businesses. The banks saw these companies as a risk. Being 'unbanked' was a grow-ing issue, and people started asking me how to get banked.

So, we identified more problems, and we evolved again.

I invested in a Perth-based bank to get in front of the board. I wanted to create a solution to help these companies who were getting unbanked. The deal was, our brokerage would compliance-check companies and their beneficiaries, and we would veto the clients for the bank. And it worked! We successfully helped cryptocurrency-based companies open bank accounts and they could continue to operate.

Even if you're starting a new venture out of an established and successful company like Finder, or something brand new from scratch, it will always be a journey of ongoing learning and discovery.

You might be taking a deep dive into the unknown, but that's the point of diving in. You'll surface with new insights, an abundance of opportunities and different potential paths you could take that you never even knew existed.

KNOWING YOUR CUSTOMER

Like all of my businesses, as part of my strategy for building HiveEx I needed to get to know my customers deeply. The best way to learn about your customer is to *become* your customer.

For HiveEx, I was my first customer. I created HiveEx as a fix to one of my own problems, which was to trade crypto in large volumes. Then I found other people were having the same problem as me.

It's sort of like method acting. The best actors spend time completely immersing themselves in the character they're going to play. Just like the cast of *One Flew Over the Cuckoo's Nest*, who lived at the psychiatric ward where the movie was filmed, or Robert De Niro, who famously packed on 60 lbs to play the boxer Jake LaMotta in Martin Scorsese's *Raging Bull*, I was a cryptocurrency customer.

I started trading, I opened accounts, I bought currencies and I even attended a hackathon in London where I wrote a smart contract on the blockchain, just so I could deeply understand it.

In basic terms, a 'smart contract' is an agreement that is written into a computer program and it exists in the blockchain forever. It's trackable and can't be reversed.

I saw the hackathon event advertised while I was visiting our London office in 2018, and I wanted to learn about them. I built a contract that was essentially a token, which is a virtual currency, like Bitcoin. You could send that token to different wallets. It worked really well. I still have the code – it's on my GitHub, which is an open-source community where you can share your code with other developers to use.

My smart contract was written on the Ethereum blockchain in Solidity – the coding language of Ethereum. And it taught me the fundamentals of blockchain and tokens.

We sold HiveEx two years later to laser-focus on developing the Finder app.

As with anything new, I love to learn the absolute fundamentals of how it works. Sometimes I immerse myself so much in the industry that I become a subject matter expert. When you become an expert, you're a thought leader, which opens up new opportunities to promote your business.

THERE'S SOMETHING ABOUT MARY

The best way to test out your business idea is to simply talk to a potential customer. My mentor Michael Kiely taught me this strategy; it's the fundamental principle of working from the customer backwards.

Rewind to when Ciao and I were just starting out. Before Finder, it was just Credit Card Finder and I needed to find some potential customers to test our idea.

I sent out an email to some friends and colleagues and I asked them, 'Does anyone have credit card debt, and if so, are you free for a 30-minute chat? I'm doing some research for a potential business idea.'

Someone agreed to chat with me. Let's call her Mary. This meeting blew my mind and Mary's story has stayed with me ever since.

I walked into the meeting with the hope that I was going to learn more about the problem, which in this case was credit card debt. Credit Card Finder was all about helping people learn, compare and choose a credit card, so I needed to truly understand what it was like to have this debt from as many people as possible.

Mary told me that she had found herself in debt after her car broke down, and a few days later she was hit with another bill – this time for her car insurance. Mary couldn't afford it – she had maxed out her credit card and needed to find some cash fast.

I wanted to understand how she got herself *out* of the problem. In this case, Mary got a debt consolidation loan. She shared with me how she came across this type of loan and the process she went through, and it really helped me build this image of what my typical customer might look like and how they might operate.

I then decided to test my potential solution on her. I said, 'If there was a website called Credit Card Finder where you could read about cards and compare them in a table, would that have helped you?'

I had connected with her, I had empathised with her problem, and now I could get a really honest reading on my product from someone that I saw as a potential customer. I needed to know everything she'd expect from a site like that.

This was the moment in time when I got to directly ask the customer how they wanted me to build my product. It's an incredible advantage. This strategy invites your first customers to be part of your journey, and they get to contribute to the design of your product. The outcome is that you end up building a product that your customers want.

Hearing Mary's story gave me empathy for the customer. I had met someone who actually didn't see the world as just products and services, but as solutions to their problems. My perspective was flipped on its head; it made me look at credit cards differently.

I could feel the customer problem, and that gave me the context I needed to understand how to build a solution in a way that would make sense to them.

Every time I make a decision, I think of Mary and the problem she needed to solve. It reminds me to think about why our customers do what they do. If I don't know the answer, I need to go and find out.

TALK THE TALK

Self-made multimillionaire Bobbi Brown credits the success of her make-up empire to talking to anyone and everyone who would listen.

I first heard Bobbi's inspiring story in 2015 when she shared her journey at an event in Sydney. I was inspired. Bobbi pivoted from make-up artist to cosmetics brand owner after developing a nude lipstick with a local New York chemist. Bobbi saw a gap in the market and took a bold risk to make something that wasn't done before.

Later, in a 2017 interview, Bobbi explained how it all started when she was just one year out of college and an aspiring make-up artist. Bobbi didn't know anyone and simply hit the *Yellow Pages*, cold calling everyone that came up under the terms 'make-up' and 'model'.

The next game-changing conversation Bobbi had was when she met a woman in the elevator of her apartment building. Bobbi has a rule about always saying hello to people in elevators – this is key to manufacturing serendipity!

The woman worked at a lab in Long Island, and that opened the door to Bobbi producing her lipstick line from that lab. Even when

Bobbi eventually sold the company, she insisted the lipsticks must still be made at the local facility.

Talking to people is great for researching and building your idea, and you should never underestimate the serendipity that could come from one conversation with the right person.

DOORDASH DOLLARS

DoorDash is another great example of how talking to people can really catapult you forward. It's an American-based food delivery company, much like Menulog and UberEats. As of March 2021, it's worth US$42.97 billion.

In the beginning, the founders were just four entrepreneurs looking for a problem. It was 2012 and they approached a bunch of different local restaurants, asking what problems and issues were regularly coming up for them in their day-to-day operations.

The first woman who flagged the problem of deliveries was running a bakery selling macaroons. The four entrepreneurs were actually putting a different business idea in front of her at the time, but as they were leaving, she pulled out a huge book of orders – this booklet was thick! She said, 'Do you know how you could really help me?'

They did a little more research and found a lot of other restaurants and food businesses in the area were having a similar problem – they couldn't get their food out to customers. The delivery system in the Bay Area needed an overhaul.

They went back to the drawing board and built a new restaurant delivery website called paloaltodelivery.com. The entrepreneurs personally took people's food orders, collected the food and delivered the orders. They 'were students by day, delivery drivers by night'.

They got this bonus opportunity to deeply understand the problem they were trying to solve by personally doing the delivery driving. They kept talking to people. They kept learning about the problems and understanding their customers, so they could keep improving their product.

To this day, the DoorDash website still pledges: 'We learned so much as drivers that we now have every team member start as a driver in their first week at our company.'

That is how manufactured serendipity changed the way we get our food across the globe forever.

PRACTISING WHAT I PREACH

I make it my mission to continually get in front of the customer and talk to them. I recently found myself in front of some more potential customers, just like Mary, and I asked them why they did – or didn't – use Finder.

These particular customers didn't use our website. They explained that they found the process difficult: going to Google, searching for Finder, opening the website and entering in a whole stack of details. I agreed with them. I imagined those customers sitting on the couch at 9:15pm on a Thursday night once the kids finally went to bed, and deciding they couldn't be bothered going through that process.

The 'can't be bothered' attitude is one of the biggest issues facing our business to date. But the magic in getting that feedback was how the Finder app started.

The app is now a place that connects your bank accounts, credit cards and loans, and automatically compares your products and alerts you to deals that could save you money. You can also buy and sell Bitcoin.

The key to discovering places to grow your business is to talk to people who *are not* your customers. Discover the reasons why they don't purchase your product, and try to solve those challenges and problems to expand your customer base by innovating and creating new things for them.

> **'The key to discovering places to grow your business is to talk to people who are not your customers.'**
>
> Fred Schebesta

Without speaking to these non-consumers of your product, you have no chance to innovate something new.

IS THERE A MARKET IN THE GAP?

It's one thing to find a gap in the market, but it's another to know whether there's a *market* in the *gap*. Shoes of Prey is a real-life example of this.

Shoes of Prey was an Australian shoe personalisation company, which closed in March 2019 after 10 years of growth. It had some big-name investors like Atlassian founder Mike Cannon-Brookes, Bill Tai, and venture capital firms Blue Sky, Greycroft and Blackbird Ventures.

Its premise was to give you a platform to design your own shoes. Every woman's dream, right? Wrong.

Shoes of Prey created a product that the mass market didn't really want. The company's initial success was thanks to a niche group of customers who wanted to design their own shoes. But crucially, they were also willing to pay a premium and wait weeks for them to be made and delivered.

So, there was a gap in the market, because there was no mainstream personalised shoe company that existed before. But unfortunately,

'THERE'S A GAP IN THE MARKET – BUT IS THERE A MARKET IN THE GAP?'

FRED SCHEBESTA

there was also no market in that gap. Custom businesses are very hard to scale, even if there is some initial success from a niche market.

The same was true of HiveEx: as a crypto brokerage, it wouldn't have mass appeal. It was servicing a small, niche market. And that was okay, because we knew this from the beginning. Small businesses can be beautiful in their own right.

Johnson & Johnson have more than 250 businesses, some of them with $10 million of revenue and some with billions – but all of them are the right size for their market. You need to find your right size and match investment.

Be accepting of your business and what it is today. That doesn't mean you can't pivot and grow, but it's about empathy and realism of who you are and what your business is – and putting the correct amount of investment and capital behind it.

PAINKILLER OR VITAMIN?

Another strategy to consider is the 'painkiller' versus 'vitamin' effect. I first heard about this idea many years ago at a conference.

The speaker insisted startups should try to be 'painkillers' – something you need – rather than a 'vitamin', which is a nice-to-have product.

My most successful ventures have come from trying to find the solution to a problem that people *need*. It's a good place to start, but ultimately a vitamin is where you want to end up.

The difference is going from a paracetamol or aspirin to a vitamin. This is because you're not likely to take aspirin every day, but you *are* more likely to take vitamin C every day and develop that as a habit. That's the evolution you want to make.

It's kind of like when you go from just being a demand, to offering value to people. Amazon Prime is a perfect example. You don't need Amazon Prime, but you want it. It adds value to your life. It gives you convenience.

Another example is an ATM: you don't *need* an ATM. You could go to a bank. But the convenience of accessing your cash 24/7 is very appealing. And people pay premiums for convenience.

That's what you're essentially doing when you evolve from a 'painkiller' to a 'vitamin': you're turning something from a utility into a discretion.

Take mobile phones. Initially they were something we all needed, but the state-of-the-art camera and apps that can help us be more productive, entertain us and track our exercise and sleep are something we all want.

Another great example is luxury watches. They started as a 'painkiller' because people needed to tell the time. Now watches tell you a lot more than just the time. They also tell people your status.

You don't have to evolve into a 'vitamin'. There are many, many evolutions you can go to. In fact, there is lots of utility in remaining a 'painkiller'. Google, for example, is still fundamentally a great utility.

MAKE YOUR OWN LUCK

Everyone tells that story of when this person met that person and it was such a chance event – that is what you're trying to create. When you manufacture serendipity, you're trying to create those chance events.

It's about wandering and exploring and learning and seeking and listening and reading and interpreting and reflecting on things that are outside of your comfort zone, things you don't normally look at, and manufacturing serendipity from it.

When I was asked to do a talk in Adelaide, South Australia, in 2016, it turned out to be one of the best events I had ever attended. At first, I wasn't keen on going. I didn't want to travel across Australia to a smaller city to talk about SEO when I didn't see any real direct value – I'm not selling SEO. But I still went and did this talk on SEO.

Just by chance, I met a Google engineer at the event and we sat down for a chat. He triggered a thought in my mind that I would never have realised. Unless I went to that conference, unless I asked that question, unless he was there and prepared and willing in this environment to talk openly, the serendipity that comes from being around those types of people, and from discussing those ideas, that was the gold!

That idea from my chat with that Google engineer massively helped us. It helped me unpack some really key concepts to expand Finder around the world.

That was the manufactured serendipity that came from doing something that I didn't really want to do – but actually turned out to be incredible.

PRINCIPLE 6

Be remarkable

'Extremism in the pursuit of remarkability is no sin.
In fact, it's practically a requirement.'

SETH GODIN

I WAS IN A MEETING ONE DAY, and someone said, 'We've done $20,000 revenue'. I replied, 'Imagine when we hit $200,000?'

It was possible. It was feasible. But at the time, we were making around $20,000 to $30,000 a month in revenue. Six-figure monthly profits (and beyond) seemed very, very far away.

'Imagine what that feels like and what that looks like,' I added. 'Now, what is needed to go from here to there?'

Suddenly, the people in the meeting had two options: they could either subscribe to the idea that it was impossible and continue to build an average product, or they could be inspired and think creatively about how we can actually achieve something remarkable.

How can we get to that place? This is my Principle 6: be remarkable. That is where creativity begins.

Your current level of thinking, along with the tools and resources you already have, are not going to get you to where you need to be. You have to exceed that. That is how you will be remarkable.

It's ideation, and it's probably the most uncomfortable step in the process of developing your business idea. It's also where you've most likely given up before. This is the step where you realise what your idea *could* be. It's also the step where your vision becomes a reality.

Why is it so uncomfortable? Why do so many people quit at this stage? It's because there are going to be a lot of unknowns. You're going to start mapping out your idea, yet there are still no guarantees that it will work. But if you are aiming for 'remarkable', you will find a way to succeed.

'BE REMARKABLE.
THAT IS WHERE
CREATIVITY
BEGINS.'

FRED SCHEBESTA

Remarkability commands attention. It's surprising and worth mentioning. If something is remarkable, you want to tell your friends about it.

Marketing guru Seth Godin says, 'Remarkability lies in the edges. The biggest, fastest, slowest, richest, easiest, most difficult. It doesn't always matter which edge; more that you're at (or beyond) the edge.'

To me, being remarkable is non-negotiable. It's about surprising and delighting your customers, and leaving something behind that's worth talking about. To build remarkability, you need to constantly be thinking about what *could* be.

SHOOT YOUR SHOT

I use a Vision Document every time I come up with a new idea. A Vision Document is a place to manifest your idea and map it out in as much detail as you possibly can. It forces you to think deeper about your idea and gives it life.

That's the beauty of a Vision Doc, especially if you've not written down your idea before. It allows others to see your idea on paper.

I strongly believe that a well-executed *good* idea is better than a poorly executed *great* idea. There's something really exciting about putting pen to paper and actually seeing your idea materialise in front of your eyes.

I've written Vision Docs for as long as I can remember. I spend a lot of time in the future: I think about the future and where we're going as a society. The other day, I came across a Vision Doc that I wrote in 2010 and thought, wow, that's what we set out to do! That was a really cool moment – almost like I had left myself a time capsule of the current trends and could see how far we could come.

When people ask me what they should do next, I tell them to write it down in a Vision Document. It's the same concept as painting a picture of where you're trying to go. It includes your research on the idea, why you want to do it and what you expect to achieve. I teach my method of writing a Vision Doc in my online course.

My crew is probably getting used to the constant ideas I throw around, but normally the feedback I get when I present a Vision Doc is, 'That's a long way to go, you know, we're focused on *this* today.'

But I tell them this is what we're going towards, this is what's going to happen in the future. It's why you're doing what you're doing now; this is what's going to happen next and what we're going to do about it. Then they are ready for it, better prepared, and they find comfort in what they're doing day to day, because they have a reason – they have a rationale as to why.

People want to feel motivated. I think motivation comes from a sense of purpose. It comes from knowing exactly why you're doing what you're doing. Ultimately, when you know why you're doing something, you can course-correct yourself. This allows people to measure themselves and their performance.

WHAT MAKES YOUR IDEA UNIQUE?

To be remarkable, you need to have a USP. I think it's crucial to have your USP in mind at the very beginning of developing your business idea.

You want to be uniquely compelling to your customers and solve their problems. You don't have to *be* unique, you just have to solve their problem uniquely well. That's ultimately what matters: solving customers' problems.

If you can solve a customer's problem in a unique way, that's even better. Then you really stand out! But over time, people are going to replicate and copy you. That's just going to happen. The key is to move fast enough that people can't easily replicate you, because once you finish something, you've moved forward and gone on to the next thing. That's what creates a moat around your business – a protective barrier that can't be penetrated. That's what creates the defence. It's about speed.

This is the time to start thinking like the customer. What do they expect? How can you surprise and delight them? Here are some examples of businesses that do something uniquely different and remarkable.

'Think like the customer. What do they expect? How can you surprise and delight them?'

Fred Schebesta

1. The 'under-promise and over-deliver'

There's a great burger chain in the US called Five Guys. Sure, there are a lot of great burger chains, so what makes this one stand out? Five Guys doesn't actually spend a lot of money on advertising, but it has done its research. What it discovered is that customers love the extra chips at the bottom of the takeaway bag; you know, the ones that spill out? So, as part of its business model, it puts extra chips at the bottom of the bag. In every order. It's genius.

2. The 'niche market'

Your USP might be that you cater to a niche market – just like this company called Nerd Fitness that targets 'nerds, misfits and mutants'. I love this angle. It is clearly targeting people who feel out of place in a mainstream gym.

3. The 'social good'

Australian toilet paper company Who Gives a Crap found a unique way to support a cause. With over two billion people in the world lacking access to a toilet, the organisation puts 50 percent of its profits towards building toilets and other sanitation initiatives in third-world countries. Who Gives a Crap doubled down on its USP: not only does it support an important cause, but its product is also different to its competitors, in that it uses recycled paper for packaging instead of plastic. And its company name is funny but also meaningful. That's a winning formula!

4. The 'fairer product'

Investment app Robinhood launched in 2015 with a mission to 'democratise finances for all'. Founders Vladimir Tenev and Baiju Bhatt wanted to build a trading platform that allowed the retail market – everyday consumers like you and me – to be able to access commission-free trading in the same way that big institutional investors can. At the time, it was the pioneer in commission-free trading. They did something that no one else was doing, and they built a product that was based on a fairer model that stood up for consumers.

What can you do to make your idea stand out, to gain the competitive advantage and solve your customer's problem in a new, better, more unique or more meaningful way?

SCALE TO NEW HEIGHTS

Another key trait of a remarkable brand is its ability to scale.

One of the reasons I think Finder is so successful is because it's extremely scalable. We started with credit cards, and we kept adding new categories of products to compare; now it's a go-to place on the internet comparing nearly everything for everyone.

While Finder helps people save money, it makes money while we sleep because it's on the internet and its doors are open 24/7.

'A WELL-EXECUTED GOOD IDEA IS BETTER THAN A POORLY EXECUTED GREAT IDEA.'

FRED SCHEBESTA

You can browse shopping deals, improve your financial literacy, apply for a loan, invest in the share market, buy some Bitcoin or book a holiday at any time of the day or night.

When I think about scalability, I consider a few things. One of those is: how can I build a product that's not solely reliant on people? All businesses have people inside them, but a truly scalable idea can be running and making money automatically. That is a remarkable thing to do.

My first business, Freestyle Media, was entirely people-reliant. We were building websites for other people, so we were selling hours of our time. That model wasn't scalable, and this was one of the biggest lessons I've learnt.

The moment I realised it wasn't scalable was when I found myself constantly pedalling. Every single month was a struggle. I was pitching to get new business, and then doing the work. I didn't stop. I vowed never to do that again.

It *is* possible to have a successful business that isn't scalable. However, from my experience, finding a scalable business model is a much easier way to grow than one that isn't. It's just going to be harder to grow a business that isn't scalable.

Breaking your product or service down into just one unit is going to give you a good idea if it's scalable. This is called unit economics. How much will it cost to create one unit of the product and deliver it to just one customer? Is there profit?

What you want to see at the end of those sums are some big, healthy, juicy margins. This is how you're going to start *without* a huge amount of capital, and this is also why I prefer to start small. Create some good margins, and keep investing back into the business to scale it up and to the right (UTTR).

SURF'S UP!

As the old saying goes, timing is everything.

Think about all the businesses starting out during COVID-19: the people who jumped into producing masks and hand sanitiser, or home-delivery services, or board games. Timing really was everything.

Take these two Queensland guys Lachlan Delchau-Jones and Taylor Reilly – 18 and 19 years old at the time, respectively. They had a bit of knowledge in the business space prior to 2020, spending most of their free time coming up with new ventures and building websites. (Sound familiar?)

When COVID-19 hit home soil, the boys took advantage of a bad situation. Delchau-Jones and Reilly saw an opportunity to sell crafting and hobby products to bored Australians stuck in lockdown.

It began when they were watching the news one night and a story came on the TV about a spike in the sales of brainteasers in Australia. It made sense. Everyone was locked up inside; people wanted things to do. But with the Easter long weekend approaching, they knew that if there was money in this, time was of the essence. Delchau-Jones called Reilly right away, and four hours later their business was up and running. Their Facebook ads were live by 7am the next morning.

Of everything this pair did right, going live as quickly as they did was, in my opinion, one of the biggest reasons for their success. They didn't sit on the idea. They made steps to get it on the market as soon as they saw the gap widening. Delchau-Jones and Reilly went on to make more than $70,000 in their first month.

When I think about timing a business launch, I think about waves in the ocean. These teenagers caught the wave at the exact right moment in time to see their business garner huge success. They saw the wave coming, and they started paddling like crazy!

I only learned to surf three years ago. I'm still not that great at it, but I love doing it anyway. One day, as I was out on my board trying to catch some waves, I thought about the parallels between surfing and going live with a new business.

Picture this: you're on your surfboard, and there's a wave forming behind you. The ultimate goal is to start paddling at the exact moment the wave starts to build, so that you are picked up and the wave takes you all the way to shore. If you start paddling too early, you'll be tired by the time the wave arrives. If you paddle too late, you'll miss your chance.

One way to tell when you're paddling at the right time is if you're feeling a little uncomfortable. If you don't feel uncomfortable about your first iteration, chances are you're paddling too late.

It's just like Diffusion of Innovation (DOI) Theory. This idea dates back to the 1960s, when sociologist E.M. Rogers identified when different types of people adopt new trends. It's visually represented in a bell curve, which looks just like a wave.

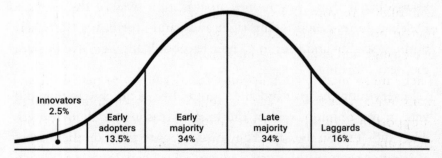

Source: Everett Rogers Diffusion of Innovations model

I like to use the DOI bell curve when I'm trying to assess the stage of innovation a particular product or service is at. It's a powerful way to help understand who I'm actually trying to market to.

Is it for someone who can handle the bumps – an 'early adopter'? Or is it for the 'early majority', so I need to smooth it out and make it really simple?

These things are really important to understand and be clear about, as they help you determine who to go after and focus the innovation towards.

In the first band are the 'innovators' – this is a very small group. They are the ones who love to be first to try new trends. They want to get the first version and love all the bumps and rough edges, and they want to be involved in beta testing and give feedback. In the second band are the early adopters. They're okay with not being first, but they want to be near the front and telling people about a new trend.

The next band contains the early majority; when they come on board is when your business will start to take off. These people don't like the bumps and will wait for a better version before jumping in. If you're launching a business where your product is new and innovative, you'll need to invest in educating your audience to reach the early majority.

The second significant pool of people is the 'late majority'; they will follow everyone else and take a long time before finally jumping on board. The last in the curve are the 'laggards', who don't like change and are the least likely to adopt innovation.

There are so many problems out there that need to be solved, so many waves that haven't been caught yet. There is an abundance of opportunity out there that is ripe for the picking, such as holograms and virtual reality, or travelling to space. If you want to start something, look for the opportunities that are already out there, and jump on board at the right time.

'TIMING IS EVERYTHING.'

FRED SCHEBESTA

BLUE JEAN BABY

We've seen so many examples throughout history of innovators hitting the market at the exact right point in time. Malcolm Gladwell, in his book *Outliers: The Story of Success,* puts it like this:

> **'Success is not a random act. It arises out of a predictable and powerful set of circumstances and opportunities.'**
>
> Malcolm Gladwell

Let's go through a few examples...

Levi Strauss was one of the first great innovators of the modern world. It was the 1850s, and Levi's two brothers were running a dry goods wholesale business in New York City. Like lots of other people at the time, Levi caught wind of the Gold Rush reaching the West Coast, and he migrated from Germany to San Francisco. Levi was going to make his fortune, but not by panning for gold: he planned to open a West Coast branch of his brothers' store and sell dry goods to the booming mining trade.

It wasn't for another 20 years that a customer of Levi's came to him with an idea for more durable, longer-lasting pants. Everyone needed pants that could take a lot of wear and tear. Levi saw the opportunity and jumped on it. He gave the customer the money he needed to patent the product, and the pair became business partners. Levi predicted there would be a great demand for these 'waist overalls', and he was right. The blue jean was born.

Levi wasn't selling something entirely new, as pants were already being worn. But now, everyone needed durable pants. Levi started paddling at the right time.

Fast-forward 150 years. Remember when social media first came about? You might have used Myspace and Tumblr. They were the pioneers. They were the first social media platforms that uncovered two things:

1. proof that there was an appetite for social media
2. that their offerings were unfortunately still a little clunky.

That's why, when Facebook hit the internet, it took off. Facebook took those early concepts of social media and made them better at a time when the industry was about to boom. If Myspace and Tumblr were for the innovators, Facebook was for the early adopters.

Buy Now Pay Later is another great example of this. Buying things and paying them off later wasn't a totally foreign service; layby has been around for decades, and credit cards essentially do the same thing. But fintech companies like Afterpay and Zip made it simpler.

Buy Now Pay Later fixed a roadblock for people who were confused about credit card interest rates, payment cycles and minimum repayments. Also, it found a market of people who weren't interested in traditional credit: millennials. Buy Now Pay Later was in that sweet spot of early majority innovators.

Gladwell says it best:

> 'We pretend that success is exclusively a matter of individual merit. But there's nothing in any of the histories we've looked at so far to suggest things are that simple. These are stories, instead, about people who were given a special opportunity to work really hard and seized it, and who happened to come of age at a time when that extraordinary effort was rewarded by the rest of society. Their success was not just of their own making. It was a product of the world in which they grew up.'

Studying where your idea is up to on this curve is going to help you understand if your venture will work. It will help you identify if you're too early or too late — or even worse, if your idea has already been and done. Abort mission if your idea is to build a new fax machine.

THE PHOENIX VERSUS THE UNICORN

No one goes surfing just to catch one wave. Every time you paddle back out to catch a new wave, you're building up your skills, your strategy and your mastery. You keep going out in the pursuit of catching a better one.

This is true even for Levi Strauss. He caught the first wave of durable denim jeans for miners. They were a huge success. But as time went on, his company transformed many times to become a legacy.

Mr Strauss himself probably never imagined his jeans would now include a range from high waisted to skinny, flare, bootcut and boyfriend, or that his company would offer clothing in over 15 different categories including tee-shirts, loungewear and genderless. But by paddling back out and catching a new wave, this was how the company stayed relevant. It's about pursuing remarkability.

Most of the time, it will be a very slow process. And that's okay. I love to go slow with carefully considered moves. There's too much focus in business around becoming a 'unicorn' – a billion-dollar company – overnight. People told Ciao and I that we would never reach unicorn status. But it never bothered us, because we were never planning on building a unicorn.

Sure, that's cool if you have a unicorn, but I want to build a company that continuously reinvents itself and survives, and endures for as long as we can possibly prevent it from dying – I'm thinking 1000+ years. This is known as a 'phoenix', a mythical metaphor for a company that rises from the ashes and takes a new form to adapt and survive.

Entrepreneur Reid Hoffman describes a phoenix company on his podcast, *Masters of Scale*, as 'a measure of exceptional greatness and rarity… that lasts 100 years or more.' Hoffman says, 'To be that kind of company, you have to plan for the long-term. You have to build resilience. Like a phoenix, you will inevitably soar upward then crash, you will reinvent yourself from your own burning ashes.'

I have seen too many startups that chase the unicorn by fudging their financials, hyping up their value and spending too much of their capital focusing on their next round of investment. These companies grow too fast and their culture breaks.

Ciao and I have always wanted to make something that lasts forever. We always think like it's still Day One, and we are going to keep going until our business is a welded-on part of humanity. It has to survive and endure. And to do this, we need to keep looking to the future, listening to our customers and experimenting with new ideas.

Sony is a great example of a phoenix company. It started off making computer RAM, then it made the Walkman, then it made TVs, then phones, and then the PlayStation. That is the evolution of a company: to go from the Walkman to the PlayStation.

Right now, the tectonic plates in finance are moving. Money is not what it once was: we have cryptocurrency, we're cashless and our wallets are in our phones. Imagine if, 20 years ago, someone told you that one day you'd walk up to an EFTPOS machine and tap it with your smartphone to make a purchase. That is wild!

I think the way to build a phoenix company is to ensure that you continuously reinvent yourself and adapt. Be relevant. Be what people are talking about. Solve the customer problem that is relevant today and deliver excellence in that.

It's also about taking big leaps and big risks that no one has ever done before. Those giant leaps are what create incredible value. They create a future where people don't realise what's coming. That is the ultimate remarkable business.

PRINCIPLE 7

Never stop learning

'If we knew what we were doing,
it would not be called research, would it?'

ALBERT EINSTEIN

ATTENTION PASSENGERS. *We've just climbed a little higher in altitude and turbulence is about to strike. Please fasten your seatbelt.*

The research phase of your business idea can feel like you're flying blind. You'll encounter a lot of turbulence and it might feel like you're off course. The plane starts to shudder, and you think it could fall apart and come crashing down.

But I want to submit to you that you should never stop researching your idea, no matter how much you think you've got it nailed. Never stop learning and developing your skills. This is my Principle 7.

There is so much to learn and so much to understand about the universe. It's actually right in front of you; you're not even aware of it. With a deeper and clearer understanding of it, you can broaden your scope of possibility and opportunity, and take advantage of that.

I believe that all the solutions are already out there – you just need to tune into them. If you can give yourself enough access to be able to tune into them, the solutions will be yours. That is your challenge.

To be endlessly and continuously learning is something that I enjoy because I love to wander and explore. I want to understand what else is out there.

So, why does this phase get so turbulent? Because it uncovers a lot of the bumps and challenges that you're going to face to get your business live. You'll get some brutal feedback, and hopefully some good feedback too. Your ideas will be flying straight back at you, and you may even be forced to head back to the drawing board.

The good news is that when you go down this journey of research and discovery, you will strengthen your resilience muscle – which helps you welcome failure and rejection, and channel it into a positive experience. It will be a learning experience.

The worst-case scenario is that you have to walk away from your current idea, but you'll be far more knowledgeable when you decide to take on your next one.

IMMERSE YOURSELF

Research is one of my favourite parts of developing a business idea. It's something I take very seriously. It can help you understand something deeper than anyone else, and it can help you cut through the noise in a crowded room.

I remember when I met Sir Richard Branson in 2013. I was at a Virgin Money event in a swanky hotel bar in Sydney. Branson was one of those people who attracted a crowd wherever he went. It was no different on this particular night; he was like a magnet in the centre of the room. Everyone was drawn to him and trying to get his attention.

If you ever find yourself in a situation like this – fighting other people for someone's attention – you've got to figure out how you're going to stand out. Everyone wanted a piece of Branson.

He was looking pretty overwhelmed with so many people wanting a photo with him. It was rockstar level. I managed to cut through the noise. When I had my chance, I said to him, 'Hey, nice hair' – we had pretty similar hairstyles at the time. He laughed.

I had Branson's attention. And from there, I surprised him by asking super in-depth questions about his companies. Questions that people who hadn't done their research wouldn't think to mention. I asked, 'How's the space company going?' to which he replied, 'How do you know about that?'

'Research.' At the time, Virgin Galactic was still quite new.

That is the level. It's going from reading the headlines about Branson to understanding the decisions and experiences he's facing in his everyday life. I asked him a thoughtful question, one entrepreneur to another, and connected with him over that. We got to talk business as opposed to just taking a picture together. I took it from celebrity puff to the real world and making money.

After that, Branson took me over to meet his CEO. My commitment to the research helped me level up.

When HiveEx started, I accidentally became a cryptocurrency expert because I did so much research into the industry. I spent hours every day immersing myself in the space.

I read articles, watched online videos and I went to as many meetups as possible. I joined community groups on Telegram, WhatsApp and Reddit. I made new business connections and contacts – and even made some friends.

I started talking the lingo and began to understand exactly what I was dealing with. I was building confidence in myself and my idea through every interaction.

I remember in the midst of the crypto boom in 2017 – right before we came up with the idea for HiveEx – I was still researching the idea of large crypto trades, and I found myself on a plane to Brisbane. Ironically, Bomber and I were heading there to attend a workshop on immersion. We were going to learn about field work from a guy who worked for the US military, who infiltrated different terror organisations and learned everything he could about them.

I was doing the same thing but with crypto, trying to absorb as much as I could in the shortest possible time. Right before we took off, I was making a trade to buy Bitcoin. It was a large trade and the whole process was so clunky. I was waiting for the trade to execute while we were ascending off the runway. I had no idea

'I BELIEVE
THAT ALL THE
SOLUTIONS ARE
ALREADY OUT
THERE – YOU JUST
NEED TO TUNE
INTO THEM.'

FRED SCHEBESTA

what price I'd locked in until we landed. It was extremely risky, but it was a risk I was willing to take to put myself in the shoes of my future customers.

In the early days of crypto, Bomber and I would spend our weekends signing up to a bunch of different cryptocurrency exchanges. We were so confused by them and their unusual sign-up processes. Some required you to take a selfie holding up a written sign to verify who you were. But signing up to all of these competitors was what ultimately helped us. We were willing to risk our own money before we risked the company's dollars.

As part of my deep dive, I also looked to the overseas markets; this was key to my process, because at the time the UK and US already had some fairly advanced crypto brokerage services that I could learn from. Then I found myself on a plane to London, ready to understand the crypto space in a new city, and this is when I learnt how to code a smart contract at a hackathon.

I knew when I was walking into the room that I was in the right place. Despite cryptocurrency being around for almost a decade by that time (Bitcoin launched in January 2009), it was still in its infancy, and everyone in the room was helping each other and sharing knowledge. It's rare to find communities like this; it was an incredible environment of shared learning and support. I love those moments.

ONCE YOU'VE BECOME THE CUSTOMER, BECOME THE TEACHER

After you've figured out how to become your own customer, I challenge you to become the teacher.

It was when I got back from London that I realised there weren't a lot of people in Australia talking about crypto, so I launched a daily YouTube series called *The Daily Exchange* and interviewed some of the biggest names in the industry.

I thought cryptocurrency was the right topic to try live internet TV, and it was an incredible opportunity to learn even more about the space. We produced interviews with some awesome people: venture capitalist Tim Draper, Bitcoin Foundation Chairman Brock Pierce, Haley Sacks AKA Mrs Dow Jones, Synthetix founder Kain Warwick, anti-virus software founder John McAfee and Bitcoin developer Jimmy Song.

When I first started *The Daily Exchange*, I thought, I can do this! I've learnt so much about the market and I've done loads of interviews in the past – how hard could it be? Then I watched the show back and I thought, whoa, that's not at the level I wanted it to be.

I started continuously watching myself back and getting feedback from others, and slowly the show evolved. I needed to bring more energy to the show, so I got a little bell – like the ones you see on the counter in a hotel lobby.

I put it on the desk, and I would hit it when I introduced guests. It was something different to the thousands of other crypto interviews online – it cut through the noise and helped me stand out.

It was important for me to be an expert as I also found an opportunity to become a teacher in the space. But hosting this show was particularly tough for me, because I was putting myself out there. It was very personal.

I remember the first time I interviewed Tim Draper. If you don't know how inspiring Draper is: he started his own venture capital firm in his 20s, he was an early investor in Skype, Tesla and Hotmail, and he invented viral marketing in the 1990s by attaching an ad to the bottom of Hotmail emails.

But Draper is arguably best known for his early punt on Bitcoin. In 2014, Draper infamously won the auction for about 30,000 Bitcoins worth US$19 million, which were seized by the US government from black market website Silk Road – that's now worth about $2.25 billion at the time of writing! There were lots of favourite episodes, but interviewing Tim Draper was definitely up there.

Draper showed me a whole new way of looking at things. He was very confident in the crypto market. I remember once, he told me that one of the categories that performed best for him was the 'other' category – the things that don't fit into any particular category. It was the things that he didn't know were going to happen. He sees the world differently and goes towards the kinds of investments that are in the 'other' category. This concept was relatively unknown to me until I met Draper.

The Daily Exchange suddenly gave us a reason to dive deeper into this industry and follow its cycle of news and headlines. We had a responsibility with this channel to know every little thing that was going on in the crypto world and help our audience learn about it. As a result, Crypto Finder is now one of our most successful YouTube channels.

On my path to becoming a crypto expert, I also found myself producing research reports, giving my opinion on industry trends, forecasting to the media and speaking at conferences all over the world. While I look at all of this as research for my idea, I also found it was an avenue to market myself and my idea.

When I was ready to launch, I was an expert in crypto launching a crypto brokerage. I could understand my customers better and had a clear vision of where I wanted to go.

MADE TO MARKET

I know you may want to get straight into producing, marketing and selling your product or service, but it's worth putting time into market research. Market research gives you an edge, an advantage.

Put simply, market research will help you understand the industry, the customers, your competitors and the trends of your market.

I actually find it hard to put into words the importance of market research, because it's something that comes really naturally to me. I'm curious, and hungry, and I'd never ever consider a venture without understanding the 'why' of the customer and the entire bigger picture.

You know that restaurant at your local shopping strip that continually has new owners and a new name? No matter what, they can't seem to get it right. There's a good chance that's because of a lack of market research.

'Just because you have a dream, it doesn't mean the dream is backed by a market.'

Fred Schebesta

There are some great examples out there of business ideas that have failed as a result of poor market research. Even some of the most successful companies in the world – like McDonald's, Kodak and Coca-Cola – can trip up on poor market research.

Ever heard of Boston Market? If you're in the US you probably have – the company's website says it has 346 locations in the States. But my Australian readers will probably be hard-pressed to remember it. The chain restaurant (then owned by McDonald's) opened nine restaurants in Australia in 2002. It had success in the US and thought Australians would respond well to the slightly more upmarket offering of baked dinners.

It lasted all of two years.

Steve Jermyn, former Deputy Managing Director of McDonald's Australia, said the amount of overhead the startup restaurant chain required meant they struggled to make a profit. He was confident their market research showed Boston Market had a 'long term future', but the old-fashioned menu just didn't appeal to Aussies.

As for Kodak, it filed for bankruptcy in 2012, despite being a market leader for nearly 100 years. Kodak famously missed an opportunity to adapt in the 1980s when digital photo and video cameras started taking off.

The 1980s was a very disruptive time for a lot of companies. It was when Coca-Cola had the idea for 'New Coke'. Pepsi had just entered the soft drink scene and Coke was threatened, despite its strong market share. Pepsi was marketed as the young people's drink, and pulled out all the stops when it came to advertising.

Despite the success Coke was having, it wanted to protect its front position. It came up with a new idea called New Coke – an even sweeter version of the original.

Coke did its market research and tested New Coke on 200,000 subjects. Time and time again, New Coke was the preferred taste to both the old Coke and Pepsi. So, it was decided. Old Coke was out, New Coke was in.

But wow, they did not see this coming!

What Coca-Cola failed to consider was that taste isn't the only reason why people buy its product. Coke was a drink that was synonymous with national identity; it was the drink of choice for soldiers of World War II. Coke is nostalgic – it's attached to memories and a sense of familiarity.

Market research isn't just numbers. And Coca-Cola learnt this the hard way – its bottom line took a massive hit when sales of New Coke plummeted.

Luckily, the nightmare ended for Coca-Cola when it quickly brought back the old Coke, renaming it 'Coca-Cola Classic'. The publicity of the controversy actually increased sales of both Coke and Pepsi, and Coca-Cola kept its lion's share of the market.

In the case of our cryptocurrency brokerage HiveEx, market research also helped us find our USP. I learned early on that it wasn't going to be easy to be a brokerage for large trades and be competitive on price. We weren't able to compete in that area. But we were able to compete on customer service, and that's how we developed our model.

JOIN THE CLUB

A key hack for continuously learning and researching is joining community groups. The amount of learning that comes from listening to people's stories and experiences and engaging with others in your industry is priceless.

I've been involved in a lot of communities over time, particularly a lot of crypto WhatsApp communities. At first, I found it very overwhelming; because there was so much noise and so many people, it was hard to keep up. But I've never met a more deeply knowledgeable and passionate group of people.

Before the crypto groups, I was part of the marketing and SEO communities, and I spent a lot of time learning and growing so many skills in these groups. I learnt how others approached similar problems. They were very creative. I would have breakthrough moments from watching people present on stage.

There was a moment when I realised I'd reached a point where I now had to start creating new ideas. This is when I became a futurist.

In 2019, I noticed a gap for a community of hustlers that was inclusive and inspirational, so I started The Disruptors' Club on LinkedIn. It's a small community of founders, aspiring entrepreneurs and anyone who wants to be inspired and learn something new.

I always hit up community groups when I have a question or want to learn about the latest trends to keep me inspired. With your product or business idea, consider: what resources are available for free to help you connect with others in your industry and get into the minds of potential customers?

THE OPPOSITION RESEARCH DOCUMENT

The Opposition Research Document is a tool I use in all of my business ventures. Finder's UK CEO, Jon Ostler, first introduced me to the framework. You can learn my method of using an Opposition Research Document in my online course.

Fundamentally, this document helps you get to know your customer on an intimate level and deep-dive into their customer experience. It'll help you go all-in and follow their journey from end-to-end. It will change your language from 'What does the customer want?' to 'I am the customer, what do I want?'

It also helps me figure out where my competitors are up to, and based on where they're at, I can determine what moves I need to make next.

I once knew a marketing agency that was pitching to work for a betting company. As part of its research, the whole marketing team actually went down to a betting club and spoke to the punters, and they made bets themselves. That insight was where they built their ads from, and was one of the reasons they won the betting company's business.

Identifying and talking to industry experts and veterans is a key part of the Opposition Research Document. These people have a deeper knowledge of the market and bring a higher-level perspective, allowing you to zoom out and understand how your idea can fit within the space.

I've spoken to hundreds of experts over the years and learnt a lot from different people in many different fields. Back in 2014, a convoy of 20 of our crew attended the SearchLove SEO conference in San Diego, and this is where I first met SEOmoz founder Rand Fishkin.

He taught me a lot about how Google thinks through his experiments and ideas. Fishkin is a true pioneer. He helped me see how websites, particularly Finder, were doing things and how we could improve.

Designers and creatives taught me a lot about the way they see the world. They innovate and translate and create interfaces for people to use and interact with and take in information from. I've always been fascinated by that.

I've also learnt a lot from copywriter Dan Kennedy. I used to listen to his courses and workshops. He deeply understands the power of words. His mastery and expertise in framing things and how to sell things is incredible.

Fundamentally, Kennedy says advertising is salesmanship in print. It's people printing words and pictures onto pages, posts, TVs, billboards, and those things market the products for you. Mastering the design, the content and the words is absolutely essential.

When I was in Chicago for the Direct Marketing Association conference in 2003, I met marketing gurus Bryan and Jeffrey Eisenberg. They wrote the book *Waiting for Your Cat to Bark?* which taught me that there are four different types of customers and they make different types of decisions.

There are:

1. competitive customers, who like to get the best product
2. humanitarian customers, who want products that are good for the environment, people and society
3. impulsive customers, who are the most likely to stock up at the candy bar at the supermarket checkout
4. mavens, who deeply research the market, read everything, go deep into every option and *then* make a decision.

Which customer is your target market? Here's the trick: you want to market to all four of them.

KNOW THY ENEMY

'Market research will not just teach you about your customer, it will also teach you about your competitors.'

Fred Schebesta

Sun Tzu was a Chinese general and philosopher who died in 500 BC. He wrote the book *The Art of War* 2500 years ago. Its principles are still relevant today and can be applied in business, sport and generally winning at life. One of the key lessons in the book is all about knowing yourself, but also knowing your enemy.

Sun Tzu wrote:

> 'If you know the enemy and know yourself, you need not fear the result of a hundred battles. If you know yourself but not the enemy, for every victory gained you will also suffer a defeat. If you know neither the enemy nor yourself, you will succumb in every battle.'

I recommend studying your enemies – AKA your competitors – for loads of reasons, but one of the biggest is this: you are allowed to be inspired by them. I give you permission! Especially in the early stages of forming up your business idea.

It doesn't necessarily mean that they have solved all the problems, because there are an infinite number of problems that need to be solved in the world, and there are an infinite number of things that can be done.

But you need to be inspired, and to see how they've solved the challenges that you may be facing. You may be able to see what they're tracking towards and how they're strategically placing their capital. You can't figure out all the reasons and rationale and answers, but you will get some sort of insight.

Then it's your chance to create something for your customer – to create something that you can defend in the future. When you're trying out your competitor's product, you're trying to see on the map what they're defending, where they're attacking, where they're strong and where they're weak.

In the same way, in most of the things that you do (regardless of what it is) someone will find a weakness. Someone will come and attack. This is truly a gift, because it gives you an opportunity to assess that weakness. How can you defend the thing that you're doing? How can you build its strength over a long period of time?

THE SUBCONSCIOUS BIAS TOWARDS ACTION

As humans, we have many biases. They are prejudices for or against something. And with any product, I believe we have a similar number of subconscious biases built in.

For example, when you see a piece of clothing and it has a really high price on it, no matter what the clothing looks like, you are likely to think it's high fashion or high value. That's your subconscious bias. I could get a really cheap piece of clothing and put a really high price tag on it, and you could assume that it's made by some fancy designer simply because of the price ascribed to it.

All of those subconscious biases are programmed into humans. They are built up over many, many millions of years.

> '(Our subconscious biases) allowed us to survive as early humans in the wild, and a lot of them remain.'
>
> Fred Schebesta

For example, humans are always unsatisfied. Even when we get the thing we want, we're unsatisfied. We want more. Why is that?

Thousands of years ago in the savannah, after hunting and eating an animal and feeling satisfied, if you just loitered around and enjoyed your satisfaction you most likely would die. You wouldn't go on to get your next meal; you wouldn't go on to defend yourself. So, being programmed to never be satisfied was a way of surviving.

I discovered this theory in the book *Influence: The Psychology of Persuasion* by Robert B. Cialdini, PhD. It taught me so much about human psychology.

I believe in Buddhism, where life is about dealing with continuous dissatisfaction and how you manage that. People will always consume new things, they will always buy new things, to try and solve that satisfaction — to fill that void inside them. Once you start to understand and lean into that, you're marketing to a person, and not to a computer or a robot or a rational, logical machine.

Humans are illogical at times. We are subconsciously biased, and we've been programmed millions and millions of years ago to take certain actions that don't make sense anymore.

Once you understand the subconscious bias towards action, you can start to market towards that and create products and services that talk to that. And I'd suggest doing it for the greater good — make a positive impact on the world.

PRINCIPLE 8

If it's not on the internet, it doesn't exist

'The secret of getting ahead
is getting started.'

MARK TWAIN

THIS IS THE PRINCIPLE that is going to change your world, but it can also be the hardest to adopt. This was the case for someone I once knew. I was helping them with a business idea. The idea was good, and they decided to create a website.

But it never launched.

Every time this friend of mine was close to launching, they came across a new idea, or a different approach, or a way to make it better, and it sent them back to the drawing board. Every time they were nearly ready to Go Live, they decided to completely rethink their business model.

It was never perfect. I'm telling you, it never will be.

Read that again.

Your idea will not be perfect when you first show it to the world (or maybe *ever*), and that's okay. To me, that's the point.

Don't be like my friend and keep making excuses. Don't be afraid to take the plunge and test your idea on a real audience. Don't be held in this state of purgatory your whole life. Don't live with regret.

Ideas that aren't executed are dreams.

My approach has always been to test early – before anything is even close to perfect. I am hungry to get my product to the market and make changes based on real user feedback.

'Make fast iterations. Get more feedback, and then repeat. That's where the real success lies.'

Fred Schebesta

'IDEAS THAT AREN'T EXECUTED ARE DREAMS.'

FRED SCHEBESTA

Too often, I hear from entrepreneurs who tell me about their business ideas and how much research and development they've done. But they never Go Live! Research is great, and it's important – but as far as I'm concerned, if it's not on the internet, it doesn't exist. That's what Principle 8 is all about.

I encourage you to build just one webpage. Write one article. Create one social media account. That's all. It doesn't have to be perfect, but it does have to be live. Worry about making it better, faster and prettier later.

It's about starting.

YOU THE REAL MVP

When Kevin Durant made 'You the real MVP' an internet sensation in 2014, he was addressing his mother while accepting the award for Most Valuable Player. In a business sense, I submit that a Minimum Viable Product *is* the real MVP – the most valuable player.

Using a Minimum Viable Product to test a new business venture is how you take your tiny seed of an idea and see if it has any sprouting potential. It's how you start small, and *test* without investing.

Eric Ries, the author of *The Lean Startup*, defines an MVP as the 'version of a new product which allows a team to collect the maximum amount of validated learning about customers, with the least effort.'

An MVP is a very small iteration of your product or service. It's the first iteration, or the first attempt of your new idea. And it's so crucial because it gives you real feedback from customers – feedback you absolutely should use.

Testing with an MVP can give you an indication as to whether or not something's going to work, because the only real way to find out and determine that is to actually put it out there. So, get it out there and see what happens.

When Ciao and I started Credit Card Finder, we didn't even have a comparison table on the homepage. Once we built the comparison tables, in the next iteration, we had no 'Go to Site' buttons, so you couldn't actually click from the table to go through to the provider. You had to click through on the review page. It was so spicy. The comparison tables then grew incrementally over time, and we built more features and functions until it became the Finder.com that is live today. This is the journey of starting out small with an MVP.

The first thing you need to do with your new business idea is identify what your MVP is. Start by boiling your idea all the way down. What do you need to simply start getting the attention and interest of your customers? What's one small thing you can offer that won't cost you an arm and a leg?

For example, say you're hoping to start a business selling cupcakes. Your MVP may be an Instagram page showing a few photos of cupcakes you've previously made, with an email address in the bio for customers to reach you and place an order. It doesn't cost anything to do, and it opens up a channel of communication between you and your customers.

Another example of an MVP for your cupcake business might be a donation. Perhaps you have a friend hosting a parent-teacher night at school, and you offer to bake two dozen cupcakes. That's a great way to start a conversation with a group of like-minded people about what you're offering. It's also a great chance to get some feedback.

When I started my first business, my MVP was creating my next-door neighbour's website for them. In the case of HiveEx, we simply went live with a website that featured a form asking people to fill it out if they were interested in trading large amounts of cryptocurrency. It was that simple. It was the foundation stone of what we did, what we were offering. It was no-frills.

'IT DOESN'T HAVE
TO BE PERFECT,
BUT IT DOES HAVE
TO BE LIVE.'

FRED SCHEBESTA

Your first iteration is the most basic. You don't need much money to start.

'What's your idea with no frills? What's the most basic thing you could do to test your idea as soon as today?'

Fred Schebesta

When we wanted to expand Finder overseas, we first tested it in Singapore and New Zealand. We knew the concept worked at home in Australia, but we didn't want to invest in overseas markets without testing an MVP first.

So, we launched the website in both Singapore and New Zealand, and we didn't actually put any products on there to compare. We simply started a webpage and we posted articles.

We didn't even update our company pages; we copied some pages from Australia that weren't yet relevant to these markets. It was a very uncomfortable experience, because we were revealing to the world the start of our game plan. We put it all out there and we were asking the internet for feedback.

There is so much beauty in going live with an MVP. Once you've stripped back your idea to a single piece of product or service, you're able to zoom in on your customers and their experience and really see if it's viable.

This isn't about making a million dollars immediately. It's about building momentum, breaking through those self-limiting beliefs, doubts and fears and just getting something up there so you can say to yourself, 'See, that wasn't so bad, was it?'

From there, you can fine-tune, pivot and adapt. The hardest part is always just starting.

WHAT'S YOUR AIR MATTRESS?

Airbnb is a great example of a business that started with an MVP and then scaled from there. Long before it was a business worth over US$100 billion at the time of writing, it was an idea for a side hustle to earn some extra cash.

In 2007, roommates Joe Gebbia and Brian Chesky were struggling to pay their expensive San Francisco rent. But Gebbia had an idea. A big design conference was coming to town, and hotels were booked out.

This is the email Gebbia wrote to Chesky on 22 September 2007:

> brian
>
> I thought of a way to make a few bucks – turning our place into 'designers bed and breakfast' – offering young designers who come into town a place to crash during the four day event complete with wireless internet, a small desk space, sleeping mat and breakfast each morning. Ha!
>
> joe

It was their MVP before they even realised it. And with that MVP, they tested an idea that they believed had potential.

They created a simple site called 'airbedandbreakfast.com', bought three air mattresses and put them in their loft space. The next week they had two guests staying over. The rest is history.

Like Airbnb, some of the most successful businesses in the world started with a very basic MVP. Uber first launched in just two cities, and customers had to email one of the founders to get a ride. Facebook began as a message board for college students, and the first iPhone didn't even have a copy and paste feature.

Now picture this: Jeff Bezos packing and sending out books from his garage. That's how Amazon started out. Bezos made a basic MVP website listing a bunch of books, and Amazon was live.

'THE HARDEST PART IS ALWAYS JUST STARTING.'

FRED SCHEBESTA

When Bezos got his first sale, he personally ordered the book from the distributor and mailed it on to the customer's address. We all know how the story of Amazon turned out.

TAKE IT TO THE SKEPTICS

Once you Go Live with your MVP, it's time to throw it to the sharks.

I'm talking about testing it out on your biggest critics, your harshest skeptics. Don't send your new cupcake Instagram to your mum who will tell you it's lovely; send it to the friend who you're scared to send it to because you know they'll probably tell you the cupcakes are overpriced and the photos are poorly filtered.

These are the people who will criticise the idea and give you some tough feedback, which might hurt but will be invaluable.

The skeptics are going to point out all of the things you might want to smooth out as you iterate.

For me, the customer is always the best critic. I study my customers, and they vote with their feet by walking to you or walking away – it's the harshest feedback of all. When we started Freestyle Media, receiving customer feedback felt like we were bumping into every single wall and figuring out which didn't hurt as much.

One of my best critics is Ciao. I took the idea of Finder to Ciao before it was really a thing. It was so rudimentary. Ciao can be a harsh critic, but he can also be super constructive as well, and I needed that kind of energy in the beginning to grow and build upon.

Ciao had so many ideas on how we could improve the site. The first thing he said to me was, 'Go Live!' I was making compromises to the site and design, and he helped me question those. Together, we made incremental progress to gradually improve the site.

Just as your first customers will be invaluable, so is anyone that is prepared to give you feedback. Listen to them. They may have an issue or give you a perspective that you didn't think of.

BEAT YOUR OWN DRUM

It may seem counter-intuitive, but I also like to start promoting and marketing my ideas in this early stage of ideation. Sometimes, I even like to promote and market a product or service before I've built it! This might work for you too. It's another way of testing without investing.

There's a method to my madness: you want to sell it *before* you make it, because that is the best feedback you can possibly get about your idea – someone pulling out their wallet and wanting to buy what you have *before it even exists*.

One business I started in my 20s was a website called 'findlostsuper. com.au'. It basically read: 'give me $50 and I'll find your lost super'. People would pay me $50 via PayPal or bank transfer, and in return I'd send them an email with a list of their superannuation accounts.

It wasn't automated. I didn't need any tech to test it out because I'd created a simple, manual process. I knew where to find the tax databases and how to use them. Of course, the business eventually folded because it relied too heavily on manual work to deliver the service to each customer.

However, it's a great example of selling something before it's built. I had payments being made and a list of customers. This was an MVP and it proved to be quite successful.

The moral of the story? You don't need to make 500 cupcakes before you try to sell them. Pre-selling is the key to testing whether your idea has real legs. *That's* the real MVP.

YOUR FIRST CUSTOMERS

Spreading the word is what's going to get your idea off the ground, and your first customers are going to be invaluable. Not only have they already demonstrated that they back you and your idea, but you can use their feedback to further your research.

Don't let those first customers slip through your fingers.

When you're engaging with your customers, try to analyse their behavioural patterns and feed this back into your business model. Were those customers who you thought they were? Can you ask them for a referral? Do they know someone else who would be interested in hearing about your product or service? Do they have any thoughts on how you could improve what you're doing?

This is exactly the feedback that the DoorDash founders were able to get, because they delivered the food themselves. They had an invaluable rapport with both the restaurants and their new customers. When they delivered the food, they were able to ask for two minutes of their customers' time to ask about their experience, why they used the service and if they would use it again.

You can do this too. Strike up a conversation with your customers. If you're communicating with them online, give them your social media handles and ask them to tag you in any pictures they post with the product. You can even set up a free online survey and ask them to answer some questions based on their experience with your product or service.

There's a good chance your first customers are going to fit a certain profile of what you expect your customer to be. Or maybe they won't. But this is all useful information. For example, say you expected a younger demographic to be excited about your cupcakes – maybe you were targeting primary-school-aged children. But then your first order comes through from an expecting mother who wants some blue and pink cupcakes for her baby shower. Baby showers! You hadn't thought of that. Suddenly you have a brand-new avenue to explore. A new door has opened up, a wormhole to reach into.

Don't disregard that information. Use it. Here are some examples of how you could leverage that sale into growth:

- Start promoting yourself in 'expectant mothers' groups on Facebook.
- Find out if your first customer has any other friends who might be in the market for some sweet baby shower cupcakes.
- Post some photos on your Instagram account showing you can cater to baby showers.
- Ask your first customer to display your business card next to the cupcakes at the party.
- Ask them for a testimonial or Google review.
- Follow up with them and ask them for a few minutes of their time to get feedback.
- Finally, thank them for their help and support of your business.

MAKE A DOLLAR

Your first customers are your new best friends. Now you need to figure out how much they cost you. How much are you going to have to spend to get someone to buy your product or service?

That naturally leads to the next question: what does it take for you to make a dollar? Take into account all of your expenses, tax and your own salary.

Once you know what it takes to make one dollar of profit, you can make $2, and then $10.

When these sums are in front of you, it may become clear which areas are important and which aren't. You might start seeing areas

'DON'T LET THOSE FIRST CUSTOMERS SLIP THROUGH YOUR FINGERS.'

FRED SCHEBESTA

to potentially save money, cut back on costs and improve your margins. This is fundamental in building a sustainable business.

When Ciao and I launched Finder, we were brutally frugal. We learnt this valuable lesson from our first business and continued with our money-saving habits. They became ingrained in us. We're still very frugal to this day, because we deeply understand the value of money after not having any money for so long.

Back then, my laptop was so old it sounded like a 747 was landing and taking off at the same time. It had no Control key. We rented desks at a shared office space to keep costs down. I tracked every single expense in a spreadsheet and made sure everyone knew the costs they were spending. We walked everywhere to save money on transport, and to get a little exercise. I remember taping my shoes in duct tape because the soles had worn away. That is the level of sacrifice you need to commit to when starting a business.

In the first month when Credit Card Finder went live on the internet, we made $80. It was the best feeling. I knew then that there was profit in this idea, and we could scale.

It's so key to focus on making your first dollar from the very beginning, because if you can get your business to be profitable from the start, it will be so much easier to secure funding down the track.

> **'Making just $1 of profit is the ultimate goal of the MVP testing process. It proves your thesis.'**
>
> Fred Schebesta

INCREMENTAL INNOVATION

So, you've made a dollar, and you've got that first bit of real-life feedback. Now it's time to use that to: Keep. Getting. Better.

That's what incremental innovation is all about: small changes every day to improve your product or service. Imagine making one improvement to your website every single day for a year – that's 365 changes you have made!

Incremental innovation is the opposite to disruptive innovation, which is when you take a giant leap forward rather than many smaller steps over time. Disruptive innovation is when a startup comes in and invents something so new, so different, that it either creates an entirely new market or it impacts an existing market by focusing on smaller customer segments.

I was first introduced to the concept of disruptive innovation in the late Clayton Christensen's book *The Innovator's Dilemma*. Steve Jobs was also a fan of Christensen's work.

Christensen sums up the advantage that startups often have when disrupting a market:

> 'By and large, a disruptive technology is initially embraced by the least profitable customers in a market. Hence, most companies with a practiced discipline of listening to their best customers and identifying new products that promise greater profitability and growth are rarely able to build a case for investing in disruptive technologies until it is too late.'

Yes, sure, you want to be disruptive. You're a startup, so you have that advantage. But celebrating small wins and simply getting better every single day is just as powerful.

You might remember the first iPod? It was Apple's first portable media player. It was bulky and the buttons were kind of janky. The next model was slimmer, the buttons were easier to use and the interface was better. As the iPod evolved, it got better and sleeker – incrementally. Now your iPod is your iPhone all in one. That's incremental innovation.

Once your MVP is live, you want to explore the next avenues of improvement and start testing some other little channels. Maybe that's Google ads, a subscription model or a LinkedIn post.

For the cupcake business example, you've now set up the Instagram page, and you've had some regular orders and lots of happy customers. Maybe it's time to set up a website with an ordering system? If the orders keep coming, maybe you'll consider hiring someone to help you make them? Or setting up a space to work from? It's time to plan your next change.

Never stop incrementally innovating. The game is to continuously develop, evolve and improve. Master the craft.

PRINCIPLE 9

Zig while everyone else is zagging

⚡

'Have courage to think differently,
courage to invent, to travel the unexplored path,
courage to discover the impossible and to
conquer the problems and succeed.'

A.P.J. ABDUL KALAM

IN 2013, when Sir Richard Branson sailed on the winning boat at the St Barths Bucket Regatta, he witnessed a famous pivot by his captain, American tech entrepreneur James H. Clark. From fourth place, he swung the boat in a different direction and won the race.

The photographer on board told Richard, 'Sometimes you gotta zig when everyone else is zagging.'

Zigging is about differentiating yourself and doing the things that other people are *not* doing. If you're doing the same thing that everyone else is doing, then you'll never create any differentiation.

In my first business, I was just building websites. I knew it wouldn't be the end place for the business, because everyone else was building websites as well. I remember when we started to offer search engine optimisation and marketing services to businesses – that was quite revolutionary back then, in 2002.

I remember always trying to figure out a way that we could get an edge in the market. The problem with all of that was that I was learning at the same time, so I was never really able to zig very well. I was actually just zagging and copying what other people were doing. It wasn't until more recently that I've been able to be more strategic, that I've been able to zig while everyone else is zagging.

In 2020, we saw the world change in one giant pivot – and millions of small pivots. It taught us the importance of being able to adapt, to change, to be agile and to be flexible. Those who succeeded in 2020 were thinking outside the box. They were zigging and they came out stronger.

I think self-doubt is something I will always have. And I think I've learned to adapt to it by using a process of pivoting. This is the way in which I've approached my self-doubt and how I've been able to overcome it.

That's why I love Principle 9: zig while everyone else is zagging. If you're not there yet, keep pivoting until you are.

To pivot is to take all of that information you have learnt in the researching phase of your ideation process and change your direction if necessary. It could be a small change in your process or the market you're targeting, or it could be a big change to your strategy or business model.

You've been testing out your idea and you have lift-off. But it doesn't stop there. In fact, all of your small tests probably brought up some issues and bumps. That's exactly what you want, because those bumps are going to give you the opportunity to reflect on your idea and think about how to pivot to improve your business.

Pivoting successfully does not come down to how smart you are, or how good your idea is, or how much money you have behind you. Pivoting successfully comes down to how much grit you have, to keep getting knocked down and getting back up again. Failures and wrong turns can threaten to block your path, but use them to pivot back onto the right track.

There are many ways to pivot, and many reasons why businesses pivot – for instance, if you're not growing, if there's too much competition, if you're not getting the results you once were, or if you just feel it in your gut.

Eventually even the coolest, most cutting-edge ideas become old and overused. Pivoting is about staying relevant.

THIS IS HOW THE COOL KIDS ARE BUYING SNEAKERS

I was at the SEO conference MozCon in Seattle in 2015 when someone's shoes inspired the idea of Finder pivoting from a comparison website to a fintech app.

This person was walking around with these really cool silver sneakers. They caught my eye and I said to them, 'Cool sneakers.'

They replied: 'Thanks, I got them from Stitch Fix. I hate shopping, so I use this platform where you pay $20 a month and you tell a stylist what sort of clothes you like. Then they send you a whole box of things to try, and you send back what you don't want.'

Mind blown!

Not only was this a cool business idea, but I realised the potential for a market where people were moving away from comparing things for themselves. They had decision fatigue and wanted someone to do the work for them.

This is the future of comparison, I realised. I needed to take this idea and use it inside Finder. I had to make a product that suited this new kind of customer. We needed to pivot.

I was also inspired when I read the book *The Innovator's Solution* by Clayton Christensen. It talks about innovation and how to grow, and the five different reasons why customers don't use your product. I found that really interesting.

One of the reasons was access. We realised that Finder was too hard to consume because we didn't have an app, and the website experience was poor on phone web browsers. People had to use a computer to use the site properly.

That's what gave birth to the idea of matching people's data with the comparisons themselves, stitching it all together. I wanted to make it easier.

'PIVOTING
SUCCESSFULLY
COMES DOWN
TO HOW MUCH
GRIT YOU HAVE.'

FRED SCHEBESTA

At the time, we weren't set up for a project of this magnitude. We needed a separate team. In 2018, we launched Finder Ventures, a separate business unit to incubate new ideas. We invested 18 months and $2 million into the app before it launched on 16 March 2020.

Great products take a long time to build. It takes a long time to create a process and craft innovations. Innovation is not a design process, it's a crafting process. You can't just go from A to B to innovation. You have to explore and wander, test and learn, try things and make mistakes. And then sometimes it just doesn't work out, while other times you find something. Otherwise, you just start again. And you go again and again, and you keep wandering until you find something.

Building the app was an incredible experience of learning something new (we'd never built an app before) and designing something unique. There are loads of personal financial management (PFM) apps in every market around the world. Some were connecting bank accounts and others were transactional – you could use them to send money to people.

But there was nothing out there that could bring together the technology of a comparison website with a database of thousands of products, and the features of PFM and banking apps. And even though we've launched, the product on the market right now is only the beginning.

Before the Finder app, people had to do the searching themselves. They arrived at the site with a problem, and filtered and reviewed their results to find the answer. The Finder app has automated the comparison process for users. We are the personal stylist for your money.

And we're not done pivoting there. I want the app to ultimately help people do the switching at the click of a button – like a personal money manager.

Bill Gates wrote about a similar concept in his 1999 autobiography, *Business @ the Speed of Thought*. He wrote that in the future, there'll be a world where everything is automatically compared for you. He said:

> '"Personal companions" will be developed. They will connect and sync all your devices in a smart way, whether they are at home or in the office, and allow them to exchange data... It will inform all the devices that you use of your purchases and schedule, allowing them to automatically adjust to what you're doing.'

Every day, we make thousands of decisions about what determines our life, and Gates believes we can support those decisions by creating algorithms, by connecting people's data and giving them the insights we've worked hard to find.

I want to create a world where people are already connected to their information, to their data, and insights are presented to them. I want to change the paradigm. It's taking people from 'I need to wake up in the morning and check Finder to see if I can get a better deal' to 'Finder has told me I can earn an extra 0.2 percent of my savings if I change this now.'

Thankfully, Finder is set up in a way that is incredibly flexible. It can be whatever it needs to be in order to deliver on what the customer wants, and we will keep pivoting as that evolves.

LEFT OR RIGHT?

So, how do you know for sure if you need to pivot?

I get asked this a lot, and there are some telling signs that it may be time to pivot your idea. It's never too early or too late to change your direction. Normally, I find the key time to pivot is when you've just launched something, because you have momentum.

You should also prepare your crew to change immediately once you have launched. It's the most exciting time to pivot. You already have an idea that has probably transformed a few times before this point to get to where it is today, and all your hard work has been building towards this point of launching. As novelist Margaret Drabble once said, 'When nothing is sure, everything is possible.'

I don't think you can ever work out which is the correct way to pivot, but you need to make little steps and little changes in some form to test the impact and measure the results. You need to be prepared to keep pivoting until you find the right direction to take. I tend to look up in those moments and look around and make an assessment, because you need some time to think and time to plan.

Rushing is not the key. Take the time to make a considered decision, because rushing is how you make another bad decision.

It's a good time to pivot when things *aren't* working. When you're putting in so much effort and it's not growing, you know you need to do something different. You know the feedback's consistent and it's not working, so you have to match what is reality with your perception of what is happening.

'The definition of insanity is doing the same thing over and over again and expecting different results.'

Albert Einstein

Pivoting is a great way to refocus, particularly in the early stages of launching an idea. By removing some of the features of your idea, you can laser in on the core business and master one piece before adding more.

We did this when we built our crypto brokerage HiveEx. A few months after HiveEx started, we launched a feature called HiveSpend where users could pay their bills using their crypto. But a couple of months in, I realised it was too much to take on. There were already too many similar products out there and the space was too cluttered. I couldn't quite figure out a unique and compelling angle, so we sold the product to a cryptocurrency coin business and they did really well.

The challenge with HiveSpend was that it was a large marketplace, and we didn't have the focus or the marketing to be able to push behind it. We had to find another avenue to do that, and we found it with the app.

It can be a really hard confrontation to face the truth when your idea is wrong. But it's great because it gives you an opportunity to create something new, to do something different. And I love that.

Here are some signs I look out for that tell me it might be time to pivot.

1. There's too much competition

Your market is saturated, and you don't have a compelling and unique point of difference to what is already out there.

If you're in this position, one way to pivot might be to consider for-going your plans to provide a 'business-to-customer' (B2C) product and transform it into a 'business-to-business' (B2B) product.

If there's something you've mastered in this space, ask yourself how you can sell that expertise to other businesses. Don't compete with them – sell them the tools you've acquired and make money that way. Turn your competitors into your customers.

Just like Levi Strauss sold jeans to the miners, another entrepreneur made bank on the Gold Rush without digging for gold. He was out there selling the picks and the shovels.

'WHEN NOTHING
IS SURE,
EVERYTHING
IS POSSIBLE.'

MARGARET DRABBLE

2. Customers aren't responding

This can happen. Sometimes all the market research in the world won't prepare you for a poor response from your customers. This does not necessarily mean your business idea is bad! It just may not be packaged right. You might be missing a human element, or the tone isn't right in your message.

If this is the problem you're facing, you need to ask yourself: what is the barrier stopping customers from buying this product or service? Focus on fixing that bit. This could be due to a range of things, like the delivery, the price or the framing. Your job now is to identify the missing link that's letting your idea down.

3. Your perspective of the industry has changed

You may find yourself in a situation where your perception of the industry is no longer the reality. If you've experienced this in your business, it's a key learning moment (and it's actually more common than you might think).

You have to pivot to match what your business is in reality, not your perception of it. This can sometimes be a hard pill to swallow, but a necessary one.

This is particularly prevalent in new and evolving industries. Newer industries are harder to research, study and predict. You're at the very beginning of the innovation curve, and that means your pivot here will be more about education. The service you need to provide should have no assumed knowledge. Your customers need to be taught why they need your product before they realise they need it.

The reasons above aren't the only ones to consider for pivoting your business idea. Your reason to pivot might just be a gut feeling, and that's also a perfectly good reason. You are in the driver's seat and you know more intimately than anyone else what is needed to unlock the next level.

'Pivoting doesn't need to mean big, grandiose, sweeping changes. A pivot can be small, incremental, meaningful changes.'

Fred Schebesta

In a way, we all should be pivoting our businesses all the time.

REAL-LIFE PIVOTS

The COVID-19 pandemic was an incredible time to test a company's ability to pivot. It forced businesses to pivot to market demand, which is one of the reasons you too might need to consider pivoting.

Think of all of the breweries and distilleries that turned into hand sanitiser manufacturers; the restaurants that started home delivery or turned into bottle shops; the hotels that started offering staycations and hourly rates for people needing office space. The Wiggles made a song about washing your hands, and a toy manufacturer turned essential workers into superheroes. All of these examples were pivoting to market demand.

When the pandemic hit, our credit products – such as credit cards, home loans and personal loans – got really smashed. We needed to pivot fast, so I started studying the market.

We created a listing service on Finder, where suppliers could sell their products directly to customers through our site. We focused on face masks, and it was wild. Within a week, we launched it in the US, then Australia and around the world. The world changed around us, and we needed to change as well.

Another reason we see businesses pivot is to focus on just one feature. You might find yourself in this position, too, where you're focusing on too many things – it becomes crowded and messy, and your direction isn't clear.

Did you know that photo-sharing platform Flickr started out as an online role-playing game called *Game Neverending* in 2004? Founder Stewart Butterfield had a dream to create a game where there was no winner, and people played purely to interact with each other. But that was such a foreign concept for online gamers that the market wasn't there. It didn't work.

What Stewart noticed people *did* love about *Game Neverending* was the photo-sharing tool. Stewart saw the wave and changed his business model to focus solely on the photos. He pivoted, and that was the start of Flickr. Flickr went on to become the fifth most popular site on the internet and was sold to Yahoo just a year later in 2005 for reportedly US$35 million.

Sometimes there is no way to predict how your product or service will be received in the real world, which is both terrifying and awesome. Terrifying, because all the market research in the world might not save you from a flop; but it's also awesome because your product or service could become more than you ever imagined if you tune into what the audience wants.

Here's another story that might surprise you. YouTube initially launched as a video-dating site on Valentine's Day in 2005. Its unofficial slogan was 'Tune in, hook up'.

It was the brainchild of three former PayPal employees: Steve Chen, Chad Hurley and Jawed Karim. According to Steve, You-Tube was a place for people to upload vlogs talking about what they were looking for in a significant other.

For five days, they didn't get a single video upload. They even offered women $20 on Craigslist to upload a video. But it wasn't taking off. Then they decided to open it up to more people. They went wider, not just those looking for love – that was possibly *too* niche.

The first ever video posted to YouTube was by co-founder Jawed Karim, who uploaded a video titled 'Me at the zoo'. Look it up – you can still watch it today. It's literally him standing in front of an elephant enclosure, saying 'The cool thing about these guys is that they have really, really, really long trunks, and... that's cool.'

It took off, with the site seeing 8 million views per day by December 2005, and in 2006 YouTube was bought by Google for US$1.65 billion.

While sometimes you can't perceive how the audience is going to interact with your product or service, sometimes you can try to, and then pivot in that direction to beat them there. That's what I refer to as pivoting to future trends.

It's going to be pretty obvious to you if you have successfully pivoted. Look out for these things: more traction, more feedback and more sales.

If it's worked, your product is a market fit, and that's when you crank up the dials. Turn up the marketing, turn up the promotion and turn up the PR. Start shouting about it.

WHEN A PIVOT DOESN'T GO TO PLAN: CARRY ON

You'll need to pivot all the time, and when you're just starting out everyone around you needs to be comfortable with researching, testing and changing course pretty regularly.

While the Finder app was one of my better ideas, there have also been plenty of times when a pivot hasn't gone to plan. But here's how I deal with it.

First, I accept it. I look objectively at the problem. I don't get defensive; I don't treat it like a personal attack. It is what it is. But it is my responsibility. I've got to own it.

Next, I determine if the problem is valid. Sometimes the problem or the feedback is super specific to one person or situation and isn't actually worth taking on board. Other times it's a monumental glitch. Both can happen, and that's okay.

In its simplest form, your idea is really just a series of steps that create a product or service. So, once you have accepted that a problem is legitimate, you have to ask yourself: at what step in my process can I stop this problem from occurring?

Great products take time. They take a long time to go through the motions of innovating, pivoting and crafting.

So adapt, don't rush in, and carry on.

HOW MANY IS *TOO* MANY PIVOTS?

There is a danger to be aware of: too many pivots. While the beginning of your business is a key time to pivot early, if you continually disrupt your crew by changing course, you're going to be hit with conflict and setbacks.

This happened to me around 2014. We doubled in size to 100 crew members and our ship was taking longer to turn. I was getting frustrated, and my team was getting frustrated with me because I kept changing the brief. The context-switching costs became very high. We were learning and trying to figure things out, and we weren't set up to pivot and move fast. We weren't set up to innovate.

I realised that this was a structural issue. We needed to adapt. We figured out different ways and made tighter squads that could handle the ambiguity and the dynamic pace of change that was required. We started to prioritise looking to work with and hire the types of people who are prepared for a bit of a bumpy ride.

I wreaked a lot of havoc back then. But ultimately, I don't regret it at all. I just had to get my team on board with the process. I started being more specific and working to shorter-term goals. We started moving in increments, not massive leaps. It unlocked our ability to maintain the startup agility, all while scaling the business.

So, listen to the people around you, and make sure you're on the same page about how much you want to rock the boat. Take advantage of being in these early stages, because they're ultimately the best time to be zigging.

PRINCIPLE 10

If you're not making mistakes, you're not trying hard enough

'I've missed more than 9000 shots in my career.
I've lost almost 300 games. Twenty-six times, I've been
trusted to take the game winning shot and missed.
I've failed over and over and over again in my life.
And that is why I succeed.'

MICHAEL JORDAN

THERE'S A SAMURAI SWORD that hangs in the foyer of the Finder Sydney office. Engraved on it is a date: the 3rd of April, 2011.

It's the day Google declared war on Finder. The sword signifies the hustle, the grit and the turning point when we consciously decided to make a better business.

That day our traffic fell off a cliff – by as much as 85 percent at one point.

It was my biggest fail to date.

I remember the day so clearly, like it was yesterday. I was in London for a wedding and I got a call from Bomber. I answered the phone in the middle of the reception area and he told me we'd just lost all of our traffic from Google. We'd gotten hit with a penalty and our pages were no longer showing up in Google search results.

Bomber was laying down all the possible theories of why we could have been penalised, while I transformed into survival mode. I always manage to stay quite calm in volatile situations – even when I'm panicking inside.

My mind went to its default: I began racing through logical reasoning and creative thinking to try and resolve the problem. We'd been penalised before, but this time it was different – it was on a much, much bigger scale. And I wasn't sure if we would ever recover.

At the time of the penalty, we were using all the tricks we knew about SEO and Google was on a warpath to clean up the internet. We were pushing the limits and testing how far we could go – doing anything we could to get Finder higher up the SERPs

(Search Engine Results Pages) on Google. But we ultimately pushed a little too hard and it all came crashing down that day.

Before I landed back in Sydney, I knew what we needed to do to claw our way back. The penalty was terrible, but it was possibly the best thing that could have happened to us.

It forced our little hacky startup to grow up. Before we went to war with Google, we didn't have a solid strategy; we were testing out different ways of doing things through a series of experiments. But the penalty told us it was time to build a strategy and raise the bar. And it all started with our values.

For three months straight, everyone in the company – all 12 of us – came together to clean up our website. We redesigned the entire site, audited and reviewed our content, made it faster, removed 'bad' links and deleted pages that weren't up to scratch.

Every single page was improved. After three months, we turned the whole business around and Google lifted the penalty.

Bomber was incredibly key in turning this around. He studied every document that Google published and worked around the clock until the penalty was lifted. It was Bomber who received the message from Google letting us know that the site was no longer penalised and we should expect to see our traffic return within the next 72 hours. He pulled Ciao and I up on a conference call and yelled through the phone, 'We're back, baby!'

We were all crying and yelling and swearing. From then on, we vowed to build the most incredible website that serves the people we want to help. We wanted to set a new standard of quality that would leave a legacy.

On the samurai sword, these words are engraved: 'Conspicuous gallantry and intrepidity while engaged in action.' It's a reminder that while our tactics can be sharp, they can hurt us as well.

CHAOS MONKEY

Failure isn't bad. In business, it should be used as an opportunity for growth.

Netflix has this awesome program called Chaos Monkey that it uses to literally cause chaos within its own systems, to ensure the company is resilient enough to deal with it. Isn't that a cool way to operate? Imagine a team of people whose job is to break things every day.

It began in 2008, when Netflix moved over to the cloud. The cloud posed some new risks, and as a company it wanted to make sure it was prepared to deal with them.

Antonio García Martínez, who wrote the book *Chaos Monkeys*, explained it like this:

> 'Imagine a monkey entering a "data center", these "farms" of servers that host all the critical functions of our online activities. The monkey randomly rips cables, destroys devices and returns everything that passes by the hand. The challenge for IT managers is to design the information system they are responsible for so that it can work despite these monkeys, which no one ever knows when they arrive and what they will destroy.'

I think the concept of the 'chaos monkey' is an incredible demonstration of why failing and making mistakes is important. Netflix is actively trying to rip apart what exists in a bid to make its business better, stronger and more resilient.

The chaos monkey is ultimately a tactic to improve Netflix's service. Your failures, roadblocks and setbacks are going to teach you, redirect you and ultimately create a better finished product.

Let those monkeys loose!

'Failing creates opportunities to take positive action.'

FRED SCHEBESTA

ALL FAILURES ARE GOOD

Just like Netflix unleashes chaos, you should encourage failure, because that means you've tried something and you can now learn from it.

I personally would *prefer* to fail than to have no result at all.

That is why I carry such a bias to Go Live! By going live you'll get a result either way, whether it's positive or negative.

If I lead a campaign that completely flops or we send out an email that no one opens, I say to the team, 'That's great, now we know people don't like those things. So, what's the opportunity now? How about we try the opposite?' Failing creates opportunities to take positive action.

There's a great book called *The Obstacle Is the Way: The Timeless Art of Turning Trials into Triumph*, which taught me all about the principles of Stoicism. It looks at how some of history's most successful people adapted the method of the Stoics, which is based around three disciplines:

1. Perception: how we see the problem

2. Action: how we use creativity to turn these problems into opportunity

3. Will: how our inner strength helps us bounce back.

When Ciao and I first started Freestyle Media, I had no idea what I was doing. I was 20 years old and I made every single mistake you could possibly make running a business.

I was hiring people too fast and hiring people too slow. I was not getting enough detail and misreading data.

I was not engaging customers enough, building the wrong product, focusing on the wrong business problem, focusing on too many business problems and not directing enough focus on a single strategy and plan.

I distributed too much capital into the *wrong* areas, and I hired people who were destructive and held onto them for too long. I was expanding too fast, expanding too slow, taking on too much risk and not taking on enough risk at the right times.

Every mistake you can think of? I made it. But where I didn't fail was my persistence. I rolled with every punch; I carried on. I learnt from them.

Fifteen years later, when I travelled to New York City to set up our US team with Bomber and Michelle Hutchison, who was our Global Head of Communications, I called a meeting with our new team.

I said, 'Before we start, I want to say one thing: as we build this business, I want you to know that it's okay to make mistakes. Because now is that time. We've got so much to learn. Go out and make some mistakes.'

I still encourage mistakes today. The courage to give things a go, even if they might fail, is what makes a great business and informs great marketing.

Imagine the person inside Toyota who said, 'Hey, I have this idea. We're going to jump up and scream "Oh, what a feeling!" to sell cars.'

I can imagine a room full of fellow marketers going, 'Ah, not sure… I don't know about that. Don't we want to show off the car or something? Or how it drives?'

That suggestion was a courageous one and it could have failed spectacularly – but it paid off.

I tell our crew all the time, 'I am not seeing enough mistakes. There are just not enough errors right now. Push it further. I want to be cleaning up some mess!'

No mess is a clear sign to me we're not pushing hard enough, we're not making enough mistakes. I want the mistakes to be made, because that's where ideas flourish and greatness grows.

So, in the position you are in right now, screw something up, and start again. Keep trying until something sticks.

EVEN BIG COMPANIES CAN FAIL

While it can be easier to pivot from mistakes and failures in those earlier stages of a startup, that's not to say you can't fail when you're a big business as well.

In 2020, during the pandemic, we had a venture that didn't work out. The Finder Marketplace was halted as fast as it went live. It was sad, but it was also a massive learning curve.

I saw the opportunity and I reached down into the wormhole. We could see the demand for information online. Everyone wanted to know what was happening, what it meant for them and where to buy the things they needed.

We were creating guides about COVID-19 in every country and updating them every day to help people find that information. As physical stores closed in lockdown, people were forced to shop online.

Ecommerce was going absolutely gangbusters. I noticed ecommerce platforms doubling their margins; internet use almost doubled and online streaming was up.

But still, only 28 percent of people in the world shop online. And in the US – which is the second-largest ecommerce market in the world (behind China) – just 14 percent of all retail sales are online, according to the US Census Bureau.

There was a huge rush of merchants that were looking to get onto Finder and market their services. We needed a really fast way to do that. So, I thought, let's spin up a marketplace.

We've always thought about building a marketplace on Finder and that was a project we had in the pipeline, but it wasn't one of those things we could easily just spin up and do. This was a moment in time where we needed to pivot and grow, and we needed a tactic.

While it was a great time to launch a marketplace, it was the wrong timing for Finder. We missed the wave. We were too late. We needed more time, resources and capital to get it to where it needed to be to launch a business like that. There were so many big competitors already out there. We didn't really have a clear and differentiated edge, either.

It was a proof of concept, an MVP, and it worked. It had all the bits that were needed, but it would have needed so much investment to build it out properly and successfully. I was sad we had to shut it down because we put so much work into it. It would have been great to be *that* company that built that dream. But it's just one of those ideas that didn't work out.

I am grateful that we learnt so much about the whole process. I learnt not to take on a massive competitor during a crisis. I learnt my lesson about adopting a business model without enough capital. I also learnt the capabilities of our crew. The engineering team is amazing! We can literally build anything, and do it fast. I learnt about payments. It was super fun to build ecommerce. I loved it – even though it failed.

FAMOUS FAILS

Even Elon Musk fails. The founder of SpaceX and the TechnoKing of Tesla has made loads of mistakes over his career. It's these mistakes that have given Musk the edge to go long, take risks and persist.

Musk famously said, 'Failure is an option here. If things are not failing, you are not innovating enough.'

Musk's first company was called Zip2 and launched in 1995. He started it with his brother Kimbal Musk, and it basically provided one of the very first searchable business directories online – like a *Yellow Pages* telephone directory, with maps included.

When they received funding from Mohr Davidow Ventures, Musk moved into the Chief Technology Officer role and Rich Sorkin came on to be the CEO. It's reported that Musk wasn't happy with the demotion and became very destructive until he left in 1999.

Musk spoke about his time at Zip2 in an awards ceremony in 2011: 'I was very naive and much stupider than I am now. I wish I could go back and give myself a slap on my face.'

After Zip2, Musk went on to become CEO of PayPal. But he had some fairly spicy views and clashed with other execs, and in 2000, when he was on a trip to Australia, he was ousted as the CEO there too.

Then came SpaceX, where Musk was responsible for three failed rocket launches. He became a large shareholder in Tesla, but by 2008, both SpaceX and Tesla were facing bankruptcy. It didn't stop him from persevering.

Elon Musk has mastered the art of failing successfully. He's now worth about US$170 billion at the time of writing.

I had to look up the word 'entrepreneur' the other day. I didn't actually know how to define what I did. The definition told me that an entrepreneur is a person who sets up a business or businesses while taking on financial risks in the hope of profit. I found that really fascinating. Entrepreneurs are literally defined by their risks and a profit that isn't even guaranteed.

I think a lot of people have this idea that entrepreneurs are reckless, but I disagree. I think entrepreneurs are actually incredible risk managers.

What we're able to do as entrepreneurs is decide when to bet against the house, because sometimes the house can be wrong too.

So, bet against the house, and be okay with the outcome. It will eventually pay off.

FEELING FAILURE

In January 2020, when we were weeks from launching the Finder app, I woke up one morning and I had lost all feeling in my right arm.

I was in the snow with my family in Lech, Austria. My first thought was that I was having a stroke. I wasn't unwell; I was healthy and pretty fit. But I couldn't stop the pins-and-needles running up my arm. Something was seriously wrong.

I saw so many doctors and underwent so many tests. I had an MRI scan, I saw a nerve doctor, I had electrolysis tests, an ECG test to monitor my heart. When all the results came back negative, I realised that potentially I might be just fine, physically. But my body was seriously trying to tell me something.

So, I called my emotional coach, Craig. I explained to him the stress that I was feeling. The problem was, I was scared.

Scared of failing, scared of succeeding, scared of what could happen. Scared of the unknown. The stress that I was under had literally seeped out of my mind and manifested in my body.

Craig walked me through an exercise to release the stress and anxiety. He got me to relax and focus, and start to address the problem as opposed to letting those stressful thoughts continue to manifest.

This is the level of discomfort that innovation brings. And every time innovation happens, it changes the world. That's why it's an incredible thing.

Nowadays, whenever I feel scared, I know I'm onto something. I know there's a chance I could fail and that terrifies me. But I lean into the scared feelings, because it more than likely means I'm on

'Failure is an option here. If things are not failing, you are not innovating enough.'

ELON MUSK

the precipice of something mammoth, something exciting. If I'm not scared, I'm probably not going long enough.

Feeling fear is a totally normal response to something unknown, and being scared can also better prepare you going forward. In the wild they call it a fight-or-flight response. Our bodies are designed to feel fear so that our intuition kicks in and we can get out of harm's way.

By being scared, your body is bracing itself for the possibility your business idea could fail. It's an incredible gift and you need to really tune into what your body is telling you. Let it do its thing – and if, like me, you get some serious physical manifestations, make sure you see your doctor.

Those nerves will be what keep you up at night, making sure you've unpacked everything, done the research and made the right modelling. It will give you your best shot at success.

After my trip to Lech, I regained the feeling in my arm as soon as I landed home. I learnt how to relieve my stress and anxiety, and channelled my energy into launching the app. Eighteen months on, the Finder app has been embraced as the most innovative money app in Australia, with over 300,000 downloads.

FRANK SENT THIS

There's a TED talk by the late author and educational advisor, Sir Ken Robinson, where he tells the story of watching his four-year-old son in the school nativity play at Christmas.

Robinson's son was playing Joseph, and when the three kings walked on stage bearing their gifts, they arrived in the wrong order. The first boy brought 'gold', the second 'myrrh', and the third boy walked on and declared, 'Frank sent this'.

Robinson says stories like this demonstrate how 'kids will take a chance. If they don't know, they will have a go. They're not frightened of being wrong.'

Being wrong is important. Robinson's words are inspirational: 'If you're not prepared to be wrong, you will never come up with anything original.' I hope the thought of never coming up with anything original ever again freaks you out as much as it does me. I couldn't think of anything worse.

> **'If you're not prepared to be wrong, you will never come up with anything original.'**
>
> Sir Ken Robinson

Terrifyingly, according to Robinson, mistakes are so stigmatised these days that by the time most of us are adults, we're too scared to make them. We're teaching kids at school that mistakes are bad to a point that we are 'educating people out of their creative capacities', Robinson says.

Our inner child is something we should always try to harness in business. Children are curious and fearless, and they have mastered the art of failing.

Think back to when you were a kid. The only way you could learn anything was to try it – and keep trying it – until you got it right, whether that's walking, talking, playing a sport or learning an instrument. Take that approach with your business venture. You're going to fall over a few times, and you're going to get back up.

Don't forget, kids learn to walk before they can run.

ADVICE FROM MUM

My mum always says that it's not about the problems you face, it's how you deal with them. This is a fact – you're always going to have problems. Always. It doesn't matter what issue you have, because you're always going to have them. Your success in overcoming problems comes down to how you deal with every situation – how

'IT'S NOT ABOUT THE PROBLEMS YOU FACE, IT'S HOW YOU DEAL WITH THEM.'

DR. KERRIE MEADES

you manage it, how you approach it, how you conquer it, how you respond.

Responsibility is the ability to respond. That's all that matters: taking responsibility by responding.

Mum told me a story once about an operation that she was observing. They accidentally cut into the patient's artery and blood was spurting everywhere. My mum was amazed by these doctors who were so calm and focused, while everyone around them was going crazy. The doctors were focused on delivering what was needed to get it done.

It takes courage and it may take a lot of practice, but it's what makes great things possible.

NEVER GIVE UP

I put the success I've had throughout my life down to never giving up. I loved playing games as a kid — chess, Monopoly, computer games — and the tactic that I kept going back to was to persist and never give up. I am always going to hold out longer than my opponent. I'm going to be right here, continuing to find ways to survive and enjoy myself.

I remember when I was younger, I used to play the computer game *Age of Empires II*. On one particular day I was sitting there playing with a friend, but we were outmatched by our opponents. We agreed to just keep going, to keep grinding, and over time we slowly came back.

It took us nearly four hours, but eventually we had taken over basically the whole map. And just like that, our competitors rage-quit — they threw in the towel and logged out abruptly — because they knew we never would. I always remember that story as an important life lesson: other people are going to give up, so if you don't, you're ahead of them.

Success usually happens for people in the last 2 percent. Yet most of us usually give up at 98 percent of the way through. That last 2 percent will feel the hardest, but it'll be where you can reap the benefits of your hard work.

Refuse to give up now.

THE FUTURE IS YOURS FOR THE TAKING

I'm a futurist. I love looking at micro trends and how they connect with macro trends to formulate future predictions of consumer behaviour and how industries will evolve. It's not only entertaining, it's also a super key part of developing your business idea.

I think there's eventually going to be a world where there'll be one app that manages all of your finances for all of your different banks and providers. It will automatically handle everything, like a robot; it puts your money in the right place, moves your money around, reorganises it for you, does your taxes – it will do everything for you.

I also think cryptocurrency is going to take over the entire financial market. Slowly, over time, blockchain technology will replace everything. The future is going to be faster. And finance is going to be so wild.

Have a think about what's changing and what's moving – what could happen next? If you can align to that, you can build your business around something that's going to happen in the future. You'll be ready to take advantage of that major opportunity where other people won't.

This is a major component of the future potential of your business. It's important to think about the future and where it's going, and then adapt to that.

One thing that is always guaranteed in this world is change. No one knows exactly what the future is going to be like.

You're going to have to go and try some things. And those things that you try? No one will be experts in them, because everyone's learning new things.

For example, I remember when I was sending faxes, and then emails became the norm. I knew that was going to happen, and I knew I had to adapt to that. We did, and other companies didn't. In transitioning, we definitely made a lot of mistakes; we'll always make mistakes. But those are really the learnings that allow you to make meaningful change.

Some companies don't change. They don't want to make any mistakes, and they don't evolve and don't adapt. And guess what? They tend to get left behind.

Think about what's going to happen in the future. What's the future going to be like? Combine your research with your idea, and adapt and hit on a major trend that's going to come in the future. If you can do that, you will be in the right place at the right time. That's manufactured serendipity.

CONCLUSION

Now that you've finished this book, I want to continue to support you. Your journey isn't finished; it's only just beginning.

I want to hear your stories of success, and all the bumps and challenges that you will overcome.

Here are some next steps you can take:

Connect with me!

- @fredschebesta
- /fredschebesta
- @schebesta

Tag me in your startup photos. I want to see everything – the struggles, the milestones, the bold decisions, the quiet moments, the launches, and the blood, sweat and tears. Let's share it all!

Use the hashtag #golivebook so we can build a community of like-minded warriors and share this rollercoaster ride together.

You can also check out my free webinar, where I share two more secret principles. Go to fredschebesta.com/two-principles-webinar or scan the QR code below:

If you've read this book and you're keen to take things to the next level, join my Go Live! Launch Program. You'll get access to monthly live webinars, articles and hard-won insights from me, resources to help you pivot and grow, along with templates and processes I've personally used to Go Live!

You'll also get free access to my Masterclass – 'Go Live with Fred Schebesta: How to Develop Your Business Idea'. It also gets you exclusive access to my Go Live! community and all of the unique content, discounts and experiences that come with it. Visit fredschebesta.com to learn more.

I want to help more entrepreneurs get the support they need to launch their business ideas and succeed. I've launched the Fred Schebesta Startup Initiative to invest 30 percent of the profits from Schebesta Ventures – including the sales of this book – into startups!

Starting a business is one of the hardest things you will ever do. But I submit that there is no greater satisfaction in the world than creating a business, developing your skills and watching it grow.

To failure, to success, and everything in between!

Fred Schebesta

GLOSSARY OF FREDISMS

At your service: How else can I help you?

Blitzkrieg: Total and complete engagement of a large amount of resources focused on a very specific goal in an extremely fast timeline to achieve an outcome.

Carry on: Keep going, regardless of what's in front of you.

Cracky: It's so unconsciously addictive even when you know the trick behind it.

Double down: This comes from blackjack. When you double down, you increase your risk to get a higher return.

Epic: Beyond what I expected. Exceeding expectations.

Fired up: I'm feeling confident and energised to take massive action.

For the win: This will lead to a winning outcome.

Get on the rocket, baby: Join us, or miss out.

Give it to me straight: Tell me directly what you think. Do not engage in pleasantries.

Go Live: A bias towards putting things live on the internet. It's about getting things done, and not falling victim to analysis paralysis and worrying about things that don't actually matter. All you need is the customer's feedback and the ability to adapt to it, to grow your product and build a great company.

Go long: Take the idea or project you are working on all the way to the most extreme iteration you could imagine in the future.

I submit to you: Here's my idea.

Manufactured serendipity: When you create luck and opportunities that you could not rationally or logically expect from life.

Next: Draw a line in the sand and step over it. The past is the past and the present is in front of you – it's right here. And the future is ahead of you. Go forward.

Next level: This is a standard higher than what you previously hit.

Pretty up there: I'm close to my maximum capacity that I can handle.

Right down the barrel: Very little strategy applied but extreme one-to-one combat, like a blunt approach to solving the problem with overwhelming force to achieve the outcome.

Riiiight up there: I am close to the personal, mental, physical and emotional limit of myself right now. This can also be applied to the maximum limit of any particular idea, project or person.

So aggressive: Something can be so aggressive (or too aggressive) in a good way or a bad way. Generally, things that are extreme are too aggressive. It essentially represents the extreme elements of anything.

So spicy: Very provocative and somewhat controversial.

Straight up/straight chat: Being explicitly direct with what you say or writing from what you think. No minced words, no sugarcoating, just straight dialogue.

Super key: A key is an idea or outcome achieved that fits perfectly like a key into a lock. It's also a tactically strong move. Super key comes from the engagement of a key tactic – you've achieved an extraordinarily good outcome.

Superb: That is a silky-smooth level of achievement.

Talk to me: Come and sit with me and have counsel; let's chat about what is new and what new strategic angles we can take to win.

Tap out: I need to immediately end what this is.

That is the level: A clarification of the benchmark that is expected to meet expectations.

Too legit to quit: I've failed too much; I've invested too heavily; I am the definition of this topic area's success. I am the benchmark.

UTTR: Up and to the right. This represents graphs that go up and to the right. That's the goal.

Very Keen: Very excited about your approach and strategy.

Weeeeeeeoooooww: Wow! That is beyond anything that I've seen before. That sets a new benchmark in my mind.

Wormhole: When you find a straight line from where you are to where you need to go, and you skip the queue. When you try and go through the wormhole, sometimes it works and sometimes it doesn't.

REFERENCES

Principle 1: Grow outside of your comfort zone

Pat's King of Steaks, viewed 8 June 2021, <patskingofsteaks.com>.

R Pausch & J Zaslow, *The last lecture*, Hyperion, New York, 2008.

Principle 2: Persistence is omnipotent

C Gross-Loh, 'How praise became a consolation prize',
The Atlantic, 16 December 2016, <theatlantic.com/education/
archive/2016/12/how-praise-became-a-consolation-prize/
510845/>.

M Popova, 'Fail safe: Debbie Millman's advice on courage and
the creative life, *Brain Pickings*, 15 May 2013,.

KA Ericsson, RT Krampe & C Tesch-Romer, 'The role of
deliberate practice in the acquisition of expert performance',
Psychological Review, vol. 100, 1993, pp393–394.

Moneyball (2011).

SR Covey, *The 7 habits of highly effective people: restoring the character
ethic*, Simon and Schuster, New York, 1989.

G Stone, *Singo: the John Singleton story*, HarperCollins Australia,
Sydney, 2003.

R Branson, *Losing my virginity: the autobiography*, Virgin Publishing,
London, 1998.

B Stone, *The everything store: Jeff Bezos and the age of Amazon*,
Little, Brown and Company, New York, 2013.

M Gladwell, *Outliers: the story of success*, Back Bay Books, New York, 2011.

Principle 3: Do things that have meaning to you

S Sinek, 'How great leaders inspire action', TEDxPuget Sound, September 2019, <ted.com/talks/simon_sinek_how_great_leaders_inspire_action>.

'The Golden Circle', Smart Insights, viewed 8 June 2021, <smartinsights.com/wp-content/uploads/2020/03/The-theory-of-Golden-Circle-model.png>.

S Jobs, commencement address, Stanford University, 12 June 2005, <news.stanford.edu/news/2005/june15/jobs-061505.html>.

SR Covey, op. cit.

Principle 4: Be the ultimate creative expression of yourself

'Gallup® CliftonStrengths + Daneli Partners LEADS™ Process', Daneli Partners, viewed 8 June 2021, <danelipartners.com/gallup-clifton-strengths/>.

P Flade, J Asplund & G Elliot, 'Employees who use their strengths outperform those who don't', Gallup, 8 October 2015, <gallup.com/workplace/236561/employees-strengths-outperform-don.aspx>.

S Sinek, op. cit.

Principle 5: Manufacture serendipity

P Hoad, 'Michael Douglas: how we made One Flew Over the Cuckoo's Nest', *The Guardian*, 11 April 2017, <theguardian.com/film/2017/apr/11/michael-douglas-and-louise-fletcher-how-we-made-one-flew-over-the-cuckoos-nest-interview>.

R Schickel, 'Brutal attraction: the making of *Raging Bull*', *Vanity Fair*, 22 February 2010, <vanityfair.com/news/2010/03/raging-bull-201003>.

C Wahome, 'How much is DoorDash worth right now?' GOBankingRates, 16 March 2021, <gobankingrates.com/money/business/how-much-is-doordash-worth/>.

DoorDash, 'The DoorDash story', *Medium*, 5 October 2013, <medium.com/@DoorDash/the-doordash-story-b370c2bb1e5f>.

D Powell, '"The kiss of death": investors in collapsed startup Shoes of Prey set to lose $35 million', *SmartCompany*, 13 March 2019, <smartcompany.com.au/startupsmart/news/investors-shoes-of-prey-lose-35-million>.

'Business structure', Johnson & Johnson, visited 8 June 2021, <jnj.com.au/business-structure>.

Principle 6: Be remarkable

S Godin, 'How to be remarkable', *The Guardian*, 7 January 2007, <theguardian.com/money/2007/jan/06/careers.work5>.

V Messina, 'How the patties are so darn juicy and 5 more secrets from a former Five Guys employee', *POPSUGAR*, 1 November 2017, <popsugar.com/food/Five-Guys-Secrets-Revealed-43633379>.

M Turner, '11 willing unique selling proposition examples to inspire your own', Mirasee, 27 April 2020, <mirasee.com/blog/unique-selling-proposition-examples/>.

'We love toilet paper', Who Gives a Crap, viewed 8 June 2021, <whogivesacrap.org/pages/about-us>.

'Our Story', Robinhood, viewed 8 June 2021, <https://robinhood.com/us/en/support/articles/our-story/>.

'Aussie teens Taylor Reilly and Lachlan Delchau-Jones capitalize during lockdown', Accesswire, 18 June 2020, <accesswire.com/594369/Aussie-Teens-Taylor-Reilly-Lachlan-Delchau-Jones-Capitalise-During-Lockdown>.

WW LaMorte, 'Diffusion of Innovation Theory', Boston University School of Public Health, viewed 8 June 2021, <sphweb.bumc.bu.edu/otlt/MPH-Modules/SB/Behavioral ChangeTheories/Behavioral ChangeTheories4.html>.

M Gladwell, op. cit.

Levi Strauss & Co., viewed 8 June 2021, <levistrauss.com/levis-history/>.

R Hoffman, 'Don't be a unicorn. Be a phoenix.', LinkedIn, 8 February 2018, <linkedin.com/pulse/dont-unicorn-phoenix-reid-hoffman/>.

Principle 7: Never stop learning

'The daily exchange: breaking cryptocurrency news & analysis', Crypto Finder, viewed 9 June 2021, <youtube.com/watch?v=CKrXtsRr4mY&list=PLUrt4pAH4g2-3HEB5fFVCs45bDjMKj-SU>.

A Munro, 'Tim Draper: what Bitcoin and all my best investments have in common', Finder, 13 December 2019, <finder.com.au/tim-draper-what-bitcoin-and-all-my-best-investments-have-in-common>.

S Ember, 'Winner of Bitcoin auction, Tim Draper, plans to expand currency's use, *The New York Times*, 2 July 2014, <dealbook.nytimes.com/2014/07/02/venture-capitalist-tim-draper-wins-bitcoin-auction/>.

'McDonald's shelves Boston Market plans', *Just Food*, 9 December 2003, <just-food.com/news/mcdonalds-shelves-boston-market-plans_id80402.aspx>.

N Shoebridge, 'McDonald's pulls plug on Boston', *Australian Financial Review,* 4 December 2003, <https://www.afr.com/politics/mcdonalds-pulls-plug-on-boston-20031204-jv5a9>.

'Eastman Kodak Company', *Encyclopaedia Britannica*, <britannica.com/topic/Eastman-Kodak-Company>.

P Behr, 'Cola wars', *The Washington Post*, 20 April 1986, <washingtonpost.com/archive/business/1986/04/20/cola-wars/0944c581-bf42-4b2f-b156-491e153b4b44/>.

B Eisenberg & J Eisenberg, *Waiting for your cat to bark?: persuading customers when they ignore marketing*, Thomas Nelson Incorporated, Nashville, 2006.

Sun-Tzu & SB Griffith, *The art of war*, Clarendon Press, Oxford, 1964.

RB Cialdini, *Influence: the psychology of persuasion*, HarperCollins, New York, 2007.

Principle 8: If it's not on the internet, it doesn't exist

E Ries, 'Minimum viable product: a guide', *Startup Lessons Learned*, 3 August 2009, <startuplessonslearned.com/2009/08/minimum-viable-product-guide.html>.

D Lynkova, 'Airbnb revenue [17+ amazing stats you need in 2021]', SpendMeNot, 20 May 2021, <spendmenot.com/blog/airbnb-revenue/>.

J Gebbia, 'How Airbnb designs for trust', TED2016, February 2016, <ted.com/talks/joe_gebbia_how_airbnb_designs_for_trust>.

CM Christensen, *The innovator's dilemma: when new technologies cause great firms to fail*, Harvard Business School Press, Boston, 1997.

Principle 9: Zig while everyone else is zagging

R Branson, 'Winning the St. Barths Bucket Regatta', Virgin, 29 March 2013, <web.archive.org/web/20130401005042/http://www.virgin.com/richard-branson/blog/winning-the-st-barth-bucket-regatta>.

CM Christensen & ME Raynor, *The innovator's solution: creating and sustaining successful growth*, Harvard Business School Press, Boston, 2003.

B Gates & C Hemingway, *Business @ the speed of thought: using a digital nervous system*, Warner Books, New York, 1999.

T Geron, 'A look back at Yahoo's Flickr acquisition for lessons today,' *TechCrunch*, 24 August 2014, <techcrunch.com/2014/08/23/flickrs-acquisition-9-years-later/>.

S Dredge, 'YouTube was meant to be a video-dating website', *The Guardian*, 16 March 2016, <theguardian.com/technology/2016/mar/16/youtube-past-video-dating-website>.

jawed, 'Me at the zoo', YouTube, 24 April 2005, <youtube.com/watch?v=jNQXAC9IVRw>.

Principle 10: If you're not making mistakes, you're not trying hard enough

'Completing the Netflix cloud migration', Netflix, 11 February 2016, <about.netflix.com/en/news/completing-the-netflix-cloud-migration>.

AG Martínez, *Chaos monkeys: inside the Silicon Valley money machine*, Ebury Press, London, 2016.

R Holiday, *The obstacle is the way: the timeless art of turning trials into triumph*, Penguin, New York, 2014.

'How many people shop online in 2021?' Oberlo, viewed 9 June 2021, <oberlo.com/statistics/how-many-people-shop-online>.

'Quarterly retail e-commerce sales 1st quarter 2021', U.S. Census Bureau News, 18 May 2021, <census.gov/retail/mrts/www/data/pdf/ec_current.pdf>.

M Mann, 'The story of Elon Musk's first company', SiteBuilderReport, 5 May 2021, <sitebuilderreport.com/origin-stories/elon-musk>.

M Chafkin, 'Entrepreneur of the year, 2007: Elon Musk', *Inc.*, 1 December 2007, <inc.com/magazine/20071201/entrepreneur-of-the-year-elon-musk.html>.

'#2 Elon Musk', *Forbes*, viewed 9 June 2021, <forbes.com/profile/elon-musk/?sh=7e68801a7999>.

K Robinson, 'Do schools kill creativity?', TED2006, February 2006, <ted.com/talks/sir_ken_robinson_do_schools_kill_creativity>.

major st
PUBLISHING

We hope you enjoy reading this book. We'd love you to post a review on social media or your favourite bookseller site. Please include the hashtag #majorstreetpublishing.

Major Street Publishing specialises in business, leadership, personal finance and motivational non-fiction books. If you'd like to receive regular updates about new Major Street books, email info@majorstreet.com.au and ask to be added to our mailing list.

Visit majorstreet.com.au to find out more about our books and authors.

We'd love you to follow us on social media.

in linkedin.com/company/major-street-publishing
f facebook.com/MajorStreetPublishing
⬚ instagram.com/majorstreetpublishing
🐦 @MajorStreetPub